About the Author

DON BRINE, a.k.a. Adam Roberts, is Professor of Nineteenth-Century Literature at London University. His first novel, *Salt,* was nominated for the Arthur C. Clarke Award. He has also published a number of academic works on both poetry and science fiction, and various other parodies.

THE
DA VINCI
COD

A Fishy Parody

Don Brine

a.k.a. Adam Roberts

Harper

An Imprint of HarperCollins*Publishers*

FACT: This is a work of parody. Any similarities characters bear to copyrighted characters and material, or individuals living or dead, are purely coincidental. Despite the compelling and convincing nature of the conspiracy here described this is *totally* not true. Honest. We have absolutely not been silenced by threats of a decidedly fishy end at the hand of the Catholic Church . . .

A previous edition of this book was published in Great Britain in 2005 by Gollancz.

HarperCollins books may be purchased for educational, business, or sales promotional use. For information please write: Special Markets Department, HarperCollins Publishers, 10 East 53rd Street, New York, NY 10022.

FIRST HARPER PAPERBACK PUBLISHED 2005.

Library of Congress Cataloging-in-Publication Data
Brine, Don.
The Da Vinci cod : a parody / by Don Brine.—1st Harper paperback ed.
    p. cm.
ISBN-10: 0-06-084807-3
ISBN-13: 978-0-06-084807-1
    I. Title

PR6118.O23D33 2005
823'.92—dc22   2005050453

05 06 07 08 09 ❖/RRD 10 9 8 7 6 5 4 3 2 1

But then it turned out that the Cunning Theory was Not So Cunning After All because it wasn't true. Not even remotely. Not even a tiny bit likely. Which is where this book comes in.

Because it turns out that although Leonardo Da Vinci didn't know anything at all about a holy bloodline extending to the present day, he knew a very great deal indeed about what cod *really* are, and that sinister knowledge is only now coming to light . . .

FACT

This is a work of parody. Nevertheless, all the facts contained within this book are in fact, factually speaking, factitious. Some scholars dispute the existence of Eda Vinci. But again some scholars are just disputatious. Otherwise everything in this book is a fact. Even the jokes are factual jokes. Factual jokes are better than docudramatic jokes, and much much better than fictional jokes. On that we can all agree.

The *Conspiratus Opi Dei* is a 'real' organisation; or, if it isn't, then it 'really' ought to be. Some people might deny that it exists. But they would do that wouldn't they? That's just the sort of thing some people do. Anyway, I just bet there really is a hidden conspiracy at work, somewhere. And why would you deny it, unless you are one of 'them'?

The secret sign of the Cod, nuzzling its snout against the National Gallery and swishing its tail with the twisting and turning of the Thames, is visible in any map of central London.

Annagrammotology is a 'real' academic discipline.

As for the interpretation of Leonardo's *Mona Lisa* contained in Chapter 14 – I invite you to check the definition of the Latin word *mōnaulēs* in any reputable Latin Dictionary. Just make sure it *is* a reputable Latin dictionary. *Lewis and Short* is very good. *Professor Snakeoil's Compendious Latin Dictionary, Home Aromatherapist and Boggle Aid* less so. Much much more on the significance of fish in Christianity and Philosophy can be gleaned from *Queer Fish* by John Schad, also sometimes known as 'John Shad', a scholar who – despite appearing as a character in Nabokov's *Pale Fire* under the name 'John Shade' – is real, and not made up by me at all. In the slightest. Really.

PROLOGUE

Jacques Sauna-Lurker lay dead in the main hallway of the National Art Gallery of Fine Paintings, in the heart of London, a British city, the capital of Britain, with a population density of approximately 10,500 people per square mile and a total population of approximately seven million people, unless by 'London' you include the Greater London Area, which has a population of about twenty million people and a slightly lower population density per square mile.

The National Gallery of London is one of the most beautiful of the many Art Galleries and Museums in London, and Jacques Sauna-Lurker had been curator of its many beautiful paintings and valuable sculptures for twelve years. He was a well-known and widely admired man, a great scholar, and a friend to the arts.

But now he had been brutally slain. A three-foot-long codfish had been inserted forcefully into his gullet, blocking both oesophageal and tracheal tubes.

This was no ordinary murder.

His assassin was not motivated by greed, simple

malice, or the need to rid himself of a blackmailer. No, this assassin was a fanatical devotee of a mysterious cult, working out the fell purpose of his sinister, shadowy superiors. The killer had killed before, and would kill again.

This killer had no compunction about killing. This killer knew that, to compunct at the crucial moment, would be out of the question. And, as he often said, failure was not a word in his vocabulary. He would often add that he had no use at all for the word *failure*. Although, come to think of it, he did have a use for that word, as a necessary component in the sentence 'no use at all for the word *failure*'. But I don't want to go off the point.

This man, known only by the nom-de-plume or as we say in English 'feather name' of 'The Exterminator' (except to those who knew his real name, and who tended to use that instead) was slinking suspiciously through Trafalgar Square, perhaps the most famous of all London's great squares, built between the 1820s and 1840s in celebration of Nelson's naval victory of Trafalgar. One interesting fact about this celebrated London UK landmark is that it is not, in fact, square. It is an elongated trapezoid of topographically unconventional appearance. Few tourists notice the fact that 'square' is inaccurately applied in this case, which is one reason why I feel it is worthwhile pointing the fact out.

Even fewer tourists, at nine pm on that fateful day (the letters 'pm' stand for 'post meridian', which is Latin for 'after mid-day'), noticed the hulking figure of 'The Exterminator' making his surreptitious way out of a side door of the London Gallery of Fine Paintings and slinking slinkily away.

The Exterminator.

He was satisfied with his day's work. He did not consider what he had done to be murder. To him it was merely extermination. He did not even consider it extermination with extreme prejudice, because, as a generally liberal-thinking individual, he disliked the very notion of prejudice. And yet extermination was his stock-in-trade. Total extermination. In a sense, his *nation* was indeed not England but *Extermi*. Do you see? Not that there is any such country as Extermi, of course. It's just a figure of speech. Indeed, there are no countries in the whole world that begin with the letters 'ex', which is an interesting observation. The closest we have is 'Estonia', which would be useful if the character were called 'The Estoninator'. Which he isn't, of course. In fact, now that I come to think of it, 'E' is strangely underrepresented in the world geographical lexicon – there is, for instance, not one single American state whose name begins with an 'E'. And most of the countries which begin with an 'E' only do so in a sort of cheat: 'El Salvador' for instance, where the 'El' means simply 'The'. Or 'East Timor', where, I mean, obviously the country is Timor, and 'East' is a geographical locator. This is also the case with 'Equatorial Guinea', and indeed 'Ecuador', since that word is merely the Spanish for Equator, and 'Equator' (since it runs all the way around the world) can hardly be called a country as such. That leaves only Eritrea, Estonia, Ethiopia. And Egypt. Oh, and England, obviously. And looking at that list, with second thoughts, perhaps there are plenty of countries that begin with an 'E'.

I may have become a little distracted. To return to my main theme, the sinisterly slinking figure of The Exterminator, flitting across Trafalgar Square. This dedicated assassin felt no remorse after his exterminations, for he did not regard his victims as anything more than cockroaches. Just filthy insects. It was good to eradicate them from the face of the globe. God was pleased with such work. It made him feel pure and cleansed, as if raised to a higher spiritual level. He considered what he had done and was pleased. 'And so,' he said, speaking softly to no-one in particular, 'I'm off to a brothel to celebrate.'

1

It was well after dark when Robert Donglan, the University of London's foremost anagrammatologist, was woken by the sound of loud banging at his front door. He pulled himself out of bed and glowered at himself in the bedroom mirror. 'Who can *that* be at this hour?' he asked his reflection.

It was nine pm. It said so on the bedside alarm clock. Robert had had an early night. Lacking anything that might be called 'a life', he had nothing else to do with his time.

His reflection was that of himself, a tall, handsome, kindly-faced man, slightly graying at the temples, or as he put it in his charming English way 'slightly greying at the temples'. The English spell certain words in a different way to Americans, although the fact that they spell gray 'grey' does not mean that they pronounce the word 'gree-y'. I know because I once asked an Englishman, one time when I was staying in London, and he was able to confirm this by repeating the word, at my request, twenty or thirty times. He was a nice man, and I was hoping to jot his name down to acknowledge him in the acknowledgements of my

book, but when I started thanking him for repeating
the word gray over and over and began asking him
another question he, kind of, ran away up Oxford
Street. Ah well.

As Professor of Annagrammotology at the University of London, Donglan was a senior and respected
academic expert on codes and anagrams. Could that
possibly be why the mysterious people downstairs
were banging so noisily on his door? Could they want
his help in solving some mysterious puzzle or baffling
rebus? He would find out in a moment, by opening the
door, and entering into a conversation with them,
during which many questions would be answered; but
first he had to finish looking at himself in the mirror.

If he were to be played by an actor in a motion
picture, and I'm not nagging here, just saying, it's only
a suggestion, then maybe a young Harrison Ford,
possibly Russell Crowe if he could lose some of the
weight. Or that chap in *Ocean's Eleven* and *Solaris*. Not
the original *Solaris*, of course, not that podge-faced
Russian bloke, he'd be no good; he's probably in his
seventies now, anyway. I mean the remake. With
whatshername, the English actress with the beaky (in
a nice-looking way) face, Natasha, Anastacia, something like that. Not her, obviously; she's a female,
I mean the man, the leading actor. You know who I

mean, very handsome. *He* could play Robert Donglan. Which I only mention here to help you, the reader, visualise the character, not to try to influence any casting decisions which as yet have not been made, the contracts not even negotiated, and it doesn't have anything to do with *this* story anyway. He'd probably be too expensive anyhow. Just as long as it's not that hideously ubiquitous Tom Hanks, with his huge sandbag please-punch-me face . . . anyway. Anyway, anyway. Hmm, hm, hoom.

Dr Robert Donglan slipped into an expensive cotton dressing gown, which he had purchased from a chain store, and not stolen from a hotel at all, and padded downstairs. 'Alright I'm coming,' he declared.

He opened the door, made of oak. On the far side was standing Inspector Charles 'Curvy' Tash of the C.I.D. He was accompanied by his sergeant. 'Dr Donglan?' the Inspector asked.

'Yes?' demanded Donglan. 'What do you want? It's gone nine o'clock.'

'I'm sorry to disturb you, sir,' said the policeman, unperturbed. 'But we have need of your expertise. There's been a terrible crime — a murder — and you may be able to help us decipher certain incomprehensible messages left at the murder scene.'

'Good gracious!' exclaimed Robert. 'How terrible!

I'll get dressed. A murder, you say? Where are we going?'

'The National Gallery,' said Inspector Tash. 'The murder victim, Jacques Sauna-Lurker, has been killed in a most distressing manner.'

*

In fifteen minutes Robert was fully dressed and sitting in the back of an unmarked police car. They sped through the narrow streets of Old London town, travelling sometimes in the bus lanes (as the police are permitted to do even when not driving buses) to avoid the rather congested traffic. In a short time they arrived at the National Gallery. Inspector Tash helped Donglan out of the car.

There were half a dozen police cars parked outside the august stone entrance portico of the Gallery, some with their lights flashing. Stripey tape had been stretched across the doorway. Several uniformed policemen were standing to attention in front of this tape, wearing the distinctive dark blue costume of the traditional British 'bobby', including the prominent domed hard helmet, which form of hat has led the youth of Great Britain uniformly to refer to their police constables by the nickname 'breastheads'. A small crowd of curious passers-by had gathered, and were gawping, although the police were not, obviously, permitting them inside the Gallery – for not only was it midnight and long after closing time, but the gallery was now a murder scene.

'This way, Dr Donglan,' said Inspector Tash, helping Robert duck under the tape, and leading him up the wide stone stairway and into the gallery.

Donglan, Tash and the sergeant made their way through the echoily deserted, cavernous atria of the Gallery. It was eerie to be in such a large space at night, with only occasional pools of electric light marking the way, and shadowy darkness all around. But, unsettling as this was, it was as nothing compared to the lack of settle that Robert felt when he saw the dead body of Jacques Sauna-Lurker for the first time.

'Oh my God!' Robert gasped.

'It's not a pretty sight, is it, sir,' said the Sergeant, grimly.

'It is a sight for sore eyes,' said Robert. 'It makes my eyes sore, seeing the sight. This is a sight that sores up the old eyes and no mistake.'

Jacques Sauna-Lurker was lying on his back on the polished floor of the room. The ceiling lights glared at their reflections directly beneath them, and gave the large, dark pool of blood a plasticky brightness.

The blood had spread in two butterflywing patterns from either side of Sauna-Lurker's head. Tash, observing the direction of Donglan's gaze, said: 'That blood, it's from two cuts made in the sides of the victim's neck, running from just beneath his ears down to his neck.'

'Ouch,' said Donglan.

'They were not fatal, these cuts; although they produced, as you can see, a good deal of blood.'

'But if the cuts did not kill him – what did?'

'There is,' said Tash, speaking slowly, 'a three-foot-long cod-fish stuffed into his windpipe.'

'By golly so there is,' said Donglan, taking one step forward. 'I didn't notice it before.'

'Didn't *notice* it? Ten inches of fat codfish tail is poking out of his mouth.'

'Yes,' said Donglan. 'That's right. I *did* notice that. Just checking. I was. So he aspixilated, did he?'

The policeman narrowed his eyes and looked at Donglan. 'You mean asphyxiated?'

'That's what I said.'

'You said "aspixilated".'

'No,' said Donglan, walking slowly around the corpse and giving it a long look. 'That's not a word. I definitely said "aspixilated".'

'You said it again.'

'What?'

'You said "aspixilated" instead of "asphyxiated".'

'Come now,' said Donglan, condescendingly. 'I think I know what I said. Why didn't he just pull the codfish out?'

'It's wedged in. The scales, you see, allow relatively smooth passage *down* the throat, but dig into the flesh of the trachea if one attempts to pull it *upwards*.'

'Down,' said Donglan. 'Up. I see.'

'He knew he was dying, choking, unable to breathe,' said Tash. '*And* he knew there was nothing he could do – that he had only a few minutes of life left to him—'

'Aha!' interrupted Donglan. 'But if the victim was aspixilated with the codfish then why did the murderer make the two cuts to the side of his head?'

'We don't know.'

'You don't know.'

'Perhaps it was a ritual act,' offered the policeman.

'And by ritual, you mean . . . ?'

'The dictionary definition of ritual.'

'I see. Well, I'm not a ritualism-ist. A ritist. An expert in rituals. I am an annagrammotologist – I decipher and study the codic possibilities of anagrams. Messages, words, clues, that sort of thing.'

Mutely Tash pointed at the museum wall. In his own

blood, the dying man had written a single sentence in splashy, red letters. It was very much a red letter statement:

THE CHATHOLIC CURCH HAD ME MURDERED!

For long seconds Donglan stared at the mysterious message. 'That, Dr Donglan,' said Tash, 'is why we have called you in at this time. That mysterious message.'

'It may,' said Robert, 'be an anagram.'

'We wondered about that,' said Tash. 'Can you decipher it?'

Donglan smiled. 'Of course. It is my speciality,' he said. He tried to add 'I am an anagram master', but instead said 'I amanana manna' and 'I am anamanna' and stopped. He smiled at the two policemen. 'Hang on a minute,' he said, 'whilst I work this out.' He pulled out a small notepad from his jacket pocket and extricated a felt-tip pen from the row of wire hoops that held the pages together. In minutes he had worked through the possibilities and turned to the inspector. 'I think the curator was trying to tell us this.' He held his notebook up. On the leading page he had written:

H! THE 'CCC' COME HARD, HURDLE A COLT

The policeman looked at this tantalising sentence for a very long time. 'I see,' he said. 'What do you think it means?'

'We need to find out who "CCC" are – or is,' said Donglan. 'And establish whether the reference is to an actual colt, or a metaphorical colt.'

'Perhaps,' said the policeman, nodding slowly, 'a gun.'

'Yes.'

'Or a horse?'

'Exactly. Whatever it is, it is clearly the key to this murder.'

'What's "H!"?' Tash asked.

'I'd surmise,' said Donglan, 'that it is a variant of "shh!", possibly a Milanese variant. Or Lyonese. It's simply Sauna-Lurker's way of getting our attention. More important is that "CCC" – sounds to me like a top secret organisation.'

'Possibly,' said the policeman, looking sage, 'Russian? Former communists perhaps?'

'It seems clear to me,' said Donglan, 'that a sinister organisation of former communists murdered Sauna-Lurker, their motives being somehow tied up with a colt, possibly something called Project Colt, or something else along those lines. Inspector, I'd suggest you concentrate your investigation in that area.'

'Dr Donglan,' said the policeman. 'Your help has been invaluable—'

At that precise moment, a woman called out in the gallery, her voice travelling at exactly 331.29 metres per second, which is the speed of sound. In air, I mean. In Helium the speed of sound is 965 metres per second, and in Carbon Dioxide it is considerably slower, being 259 metres per second. But since the inside of the London Gallery of Fine Paintings was filled with air, her words travelled the few metres between her and the others at 331.29 metres per second.

'Wait!' she said.

Donglan and Tash turned to face her.

2

The two men were looking at an extremely attractive young woman.

'Who are you?' asked Tash.

'My name,' she said, stepping forward, 'is Sophie Nudivue. I am attached to the French embassy here in London – from the Sûrité, which is a specialist branch of the French police.'

'What are you doing here?' demanded Tash.

'I have been seconded to the world famous Department of Cryptology at the world famous Royal Holloway, University of London, which is a department that is not only world famous but also exists, in a very real and existent sense.'

She turned to Donglan, and spoke to him in her native tongue, which was French. Rather than English. Which she also spoke. Although, obviously, not on this particular occasion. 'You are,' she said in French 'an academic at the University of London, and I assume that therefore you speak French. Is this so?'

Donglan, though surprised, replied in the affirmative. 'Yes I speak the French very well – yes. Good surely, it is yes.' He had ordered many coffee-with-milks and half-litre-of-beers in France.

'Good,' said Sophie, in French. 'I am also going to assume that this flatfoot policeman is ignorant of the French tongue, for he is, after all, only a London policeman and not a university educated individual such as yourself. Therefore I can use my own language as an, as it were, code – for there is something I wish to say to you that I do not desire *him* to overhear. Dr Donglan! You are in terrible danger! You have been tricked, set-up, stitched up like a kipper. It is imperative that you listen very carefully to what I say, for I shall not say it twice. Inspector Tash *will arrest you* once he has finished utilising your special code-breaking skills. He believes you guilty of this murder. But I can help you escape this terrible fate.'

'Formidable,' replied Donglan, in French. 'I think I understand of the words. But I not understand the words in the middle, step, which you to speak. Perhaps – little more *softly*, no, that is irregular word, I say, but, *slowly*, yes, excuse me, little more *slowly* and the words of the French are more comprehendingable at me.'

He smiled at her, rather pleased with himself.

Sophie looked at him in silence for several seconds. 'Good,' she said, still in French, although articulating her words more carefully. 'OK.'

'OK?' repeated Donglan, adding, in English, 'are we speaking English now?'

Tash looked from Donglan to Sophie.

'No,' she replied, in French. 'It just so happens that "OK" is the same in French as in English.'

Tash looked from Sophie back to Donglan.

'I comprehend,' said Donglan also in French, nodding vigorously. 'Like it is "the weekend" and "the to know what to do".'

'The "to know what to do",' said Sophie, rather crossly, in French, 'is a French phrase in the first place. But please, let's not get bogged down in such discussion. It is imperative that I communicate certain things to you without Inspector Tash here understanding. He has affixed a tracking device to your back. The exits and entrances are guarded. He intends to take you directly to the police cells, where you will be tried for this crime, and almost certainly put in prison for many decades. But I can help you. In five minutes I shall pretend to leave, and at that point you must insist upon going to the gentleman's toilet, located on this floor. I will meet you there. Do you understand?'

'Precisely,' said Donglan, slowly. 'It is to speak of the toilet, which is not the toilet at you, but is the toilet at me. I shall have been returning to the toilet after you to go at the toilet, and meeting of you in the toilet, yes?'

'Je vous voudrais dire,' said Tash, 'que je parle français, moi-aussi, et je vous comprends tres bien ça que vous dites.'

There was a moment's silence.

'Ah,' said Sophie, in French. Or perhaps she was speaking in English. It's difficult to tell.

'Oh,' said Donglan, in English.

'Mademoiselle Nudivue,' said Tash, in English. 'Might I ask to see your accreditation?'

'You have no reason to accuse Dr Donglan of this murder!' Sophie squealed. 'It is an outrage. It out-outrages outrage! He is innocent. There is no evidence to connect him to this crime.'

'Mademoiselle,' said Tash. 'Earlier this evening we took a number of scales from the murder-fish.'

'You took some scales?' repeated Donglan.

'Twenty or so, from that portion of the fish that still extrudes from the Professor's throat. They've been analysed in our labs. *Every single scale* has Dr Donglan's fingerprints upon it. It's quite remarkable actually – we're usually lucky if we get one or two usable prints from a murder weapon. But this murder-fish seems to have Dr Donglan's prints on every single one of its scales. You must,' Tash said, turning to Robert, 'have handled this fish a great deal before using it to kill Professor Sauna-Lurker. I mean, handled it a *great deal*.'

Robert swallowed. He turned to Sophie Nudivue.

'Sophie' he said to her, in English. 'I want you to believe me when I say I've never before seen this fish. I didn't murder Professor Sauna-Lurker, and I never so much as touched this fish. I certainly didn't – *handle* – it, certainly didn't *paw it* over and over,' he shuddered, 'like some disgusting fish-pervert, like somebody who couldn't help himself, who just had to press his fingers into the soggy, firm, cod-smelling flesh again and again, as if he were kneading bread, touching it, caressing it, forcing it through my fingers like a potter moulding clay, throttling its silvery-shiny wetness, its fishy firmness, pressing it again and again and again, slapping it, faster and faster shouting out "bad fish! bad fish!" at the top of my voice, until losing myself in a foul conniptian fit of ecstasy.' He wiped a small quantity of spittle from the edge of his mouth with his sleeve. 'I didn't do *anything* like that. I hope you believe me?'

Sophie was looking at him intently.

As was Inspector Tash.

'I concede,' said Donglan, becoming a little nervous, 'that I do know a little about fish. Yes. I have had some experience with fish, yes. My job requires it. But I did not murder Professor Sauna-Lurker, and I *never* touched *that* fish.'

'In that case perhaps you might suggest,' said the policeman, who had taken a small single backward step, 'how your fingerprints come to be impressed upon each of the fish's scales?'

'I don't know,' said Donglan, simply. 'I must assume I am being framed.'

'It's a pretty elaborate frame-up,' suggested the policeman.

'Sophie,' Donglan urged. 'Believe me.'

'Robert,' said Sophie, utilising his forename for the first time, her violet eyes connecting with his, their gazes locking significantly. 'I believe you. There is something else.'

'Something else? What?'

The woman nudged closer to Robert, as if preparing to whisper something in his ear. Not wishing to be excluded, and feeling himself entitled to overhear anything spoken to his prime suspect for murder, Inspector Tash leant in.

'Run!' Sophie yelled. As Tash reeled, clutching his ears, and Robert jumped with shock, Sophie grabbed his arm and hauled him away down the gallery.

'Stop!' yelled Tash. But fear gave wings to Robert's

heels. Not actual wings, obviously; metaphorical wings. He ran quickly. Sophie, also, demonstrated an impressive rush of speed.

3

The two of them clattered down the great hall of the National Gallery

'Down here!' Sophie cried, and jinked left. Beautiful images flashed past them on every side. Established by the British government in 1824, the National Gallery was moved to its current Trafalgar Square location in 1838 – a Neoclassical building designed by the architect William Wilkins. Within its walls are some 2,000 works, much of its collection having been moved to other, later-built, London Galleries, amongst them the National Portrait Gallery next door, and the Tate Britain up the river. But even with relatively few paintings, compared with some other galleries, it is regarded by many experts as one of the best samplings of European painting anywhere in the world. Particularly known for its collection of Italian Renaissance paintings, it also has extensive holdings by Northern European and Spanish artists from the 15th to the 19th centuries. Among its artists are Leonardo, Raphael, and Vermeer. It also has excellent cloakroom facilities, and a very pleasant if slightly expensive coffee shop, which has provided many tourists with an agreeable way of passing the afternoon until it is time for the theatre performance for which they have purchased tickets to begin. But neither Sophie nor Robert were interested in the coffee shop.

Instead Sophie pushed through a small door and pulled Robert down a narrow flight of stairs. Down they rushed, half stepping and half tumbling down the dark stairwell. They emerged into a dim hall, below the exhibition space, from where a number of doors led to the offices of the senior staff of the institution. There was no illumination except for a single lime-green glowing sign that said FIRE EXIT.

Sophie finally stopped, and Robert – not a fit man – almost collapsed with gratitude.

They were standing next to a door marked JACQUES SAUNA-LURKER.

'I don't understand,' gasped Robert. 'How could my fingerprints be on that fish? On every single scale?'

'You were right on the badge, I fear,' said Sophie.

'On the badge? What do you mean?'

'Is that not the correct phrase? Right on the button – is that it?'

'Button?'

'What I mean is that you were correct in your supposition. You are being framed.'

'But *why*?'

'Somebody has murdered Monsieur Sauna-Lurker, in a very public and symbolic way. Yet, at the same time, whoever is responsible for the murder wishes to remain hidden, secret, in the shadows, down, down, deeper and down. Therefore they need somebody to be punished, a scape-goat.'

'A scape-goat?' echoed Robert, horrified. 'Me?'

'There is a deep conspiracy here, Dr Donglan. A conspiracy that has deep roots. Deeply hidden.'

'Deep,' said Robert. 'I see.'

'Deep,' confirmed Sophie. 'Not on the surface, but rather reaching deep below the surface, deep into the hidden recesses of Western culture and history.'

'Yes, I take the force of the whole deepness thing.'

'Everything that has happened here tonight is fraught with significance. Everything is a symbol. Those that have eyes will see. Everybody else will be satisfied that the police have caught the culprit in you . . . do you see?'

'A scape-goat,' said Robert, miserably.

'But, with my help, perhaps we can make you not scape-goat but an *e*scape-goat.' She smiled. Then she said: 'I have made a joke. Do you see?'

'You mean,' said Robert, slightly puzzled, 'that you're going to help me escape?

'Yes.'

'It might be easier just to say that,' said Robert. 'I mean, just for the sake of easy communication.'

'Very well. We must get out of this gallery before the police apprehend us. And then we must locate the true murderer – or murderers. We must bring to light the truth of this terrible act, and thereby clear your name.'

'Well that would be wonderful, obviously. It's awfully kind of you to help me like this,' said Robert, sincerely. 'Although I'm sure I don't see how we can.'

'Monsieur Sauna-Lurker left one clue beside his murdered body. I believe he may have left other ones. This is his office. Perhaps there is something here that will help us. But we must hurry. The police will follow us down very soon.'

'It's a bit dark to be looking for clues . . .' Robert pointed out.

Tutting, or *tch*-ing, or perhaps making a noise halfway between the two, Sophie flipped on the electric light switch. Electricity, the fluid action of movement of electrons from nucleus to nucleus, cascaded along wires, governed by the equation (for current i) $i = [dQ/dt] = nevA$, where dQ is the amount of charge that crosses the plane in a time interval dt for n units of free charge passing along a wire with diameter A. Light filled the hallway.

Robert gasped. Directly opposite Sauna-Lurker's office door was a mural, or 'wall painting', of Leonardo's celebrated *Last Supper*, filling the space from floor to ceiling. Christ sat benignly harmonious in the middle behind a table laden with food, whilst his disciples reeled and leant away from him on both sides. A particularly juicy looking painted codfish occupied the plate directly in front of the figure of Christ. It's beady little eye seemed to follow Robert around the room, almost quizzically. It was rather offputting. '*The Last Supper*,' he observed. 'Is this the original?'

'Of course not,' snapped Sophie, annoyance flashing attractively in her violet eyes. 'The original is in the Santa Maria della Grazie, in Milan. This is merely a copy.'

'That's a relief,' said Robert. 'Because if it were the original, it would be very worrying that somebody had scribbled graffiti on it.'

'No!' cried Sophie.

'They have too. There.'

'Where?'

'*There* – on the hair.'

'Where on the hair?'

'Just there.' Robert pointed at the graffito, scribbled in red across the hair-do of the central Christ. A little red graffito, there on the hair, saying:

9 Θ ? ◉

They both looked at it for long seconds. 'What does it mean?' Sophie asked.

'I've not the slightest inkling of a foggiest,' said Robert. 'Not a clue. Not a *clue*.' He repeated this phrase, apparently finding particular fascination in the final word. 'Not a cluh-*ew*. Not a cl*oo*. Not a cl*uue*. Not . . .'

'Alright, alright,' said Sophie, hurriedly. 'You've got a notepad. Write it down. We'll try and decipher it later.'

As Robert scribbled the strange rebus in his pad, Sophie tried the door to Sauna-Lurker's office. It opened at once.

'Good grief,' said Robert, looking past her.

Sauna-Lurker's office was a mess. Papers were scattered on the floor. Books were pulled from the shelves. The desk was overturned. Blood was scattered over everything. Papers were scattered – or did I already mentioned the scattered papers?

It was a mess, that's the important thing.

'Do you smell that?' Sophie asked, sniffing the air. 'Codfish. This is where the murder was actually committed. Here Monsieur Sauna-Lurker was attacked; the cuts were made to the side of his face, and the large fish was stuffed into his throat. He put up a struggle, evidently, but his assailant was too strong for him.'

'But the body was found upstairs . . .'

'Yes. Even though he couldn't remove the fish, and had only moments of life left to him, he did not simply lie down and die. Instead he left this room. I'm guessing that he dipped his finger in his own blood, went through to the hallway outside and wrote that strange message on the mural of the *Last Supper*.'

'But – why?'

'He was trying to communicate something to us. Something he wanted us to know, but which he hoped to keep secret from the murderer. Can you not decipher it? You are, after all, an expert at codes, clues, anagrams, acrostics and monkey-puzzle-trees?'

'I'm giving it some thought, alright?' said Donglan, defensively. 'I'm sure the answer will come to me in a moment. Let my brain lie fallow. Let the answer assemble itself. Trying to force it would be the worst thing I could do, believe me. Give me time, it'll come to me.'

'This is hopeless,' said Sophie, looking around. 'This is just a mess.'

'Why didn't the assassin finish off Sauna-Lurker right here?' asked Robert. 'Why did he let his victim get out of the room and write a message on the wall opposite?'

'He must have been distracted,' said Sophie, distractedly. 'Perhaps he was looking for something,' she added, rifling through the scattered papers as if looking for something, 'which gave Jacques just enough time to get out of the room. It hardly mattered. His doom was sealed.'

'Looking for what?'

'Something well hidden. So.' She walked out of the office and stood looking at the graffito'd mural. 'He staggered out here, the fish in his throat, and wrote *that* on the mural. He knew he could not simply write out a straightforward message, or the assassin would see it and understand. So he put it in code. Then he made his way upstairs, wrote his final message on the wall of the main gallery, and died.'

'Nine-tiny-h-in-a-circle,' Robert tried out, standing next to her. 'Question Eye? It doesn't make a whole lot of sense.'

'Surely,' Sophie purred, leaning closer to him. 'If anybody can decipher it, *you* can.'

Robert's heart made little thrumming skips in his chest. Was this extremely alluring young Frenchwoman flirting with him? Could it be that she found him attractive? Were sparks flying? Was the chemistry between them clicking? Was this going to be the first day of the rest of their lives? Could it be that it only takes a minute, it only takes a minute girl to fall in love? He stopped, all his clichés used up. Now now, Robert, he inwardly warned himself. Let's not get ahead of yourself. Of myself, rather. Is what he thought, I mean.

He looked down at Sophie's well-proportioned face, with its full French lips and violet French eyes, and imaged French kissing it. Then he imaged eating French toast. Then, for reasons that were not clear to his conscious mind, but presumably related to some buried logic of the subconscious mind, he thought of 'Frenchie', the character from *Grease*. Then he thought of Olivia Newton John. His mind was running away with itself. He was becoming intoxicated with the proximity of this beautiful creature.

'Um,' he said, finally. 'I'm sorry, what was the question again?'

'*Can* you decipher it?' she repeated.

'Um,' he said.

'That's what I thought,' she said sharply. 'Well, if you can't perhaps there is somebody in this city who can. Indeed – perhaps Monsieur Sauna-Lurker was giving us a clue as to that person's identity.' She pointed at the mural again.

Next to the figure of the Christ was Thomas, with his hand raised beside his face and his finger pointing straight up. To this, dying Sauna-Lurker had added a single curving line, like a mirror-image of a question mark. *It looks*, thought Robert, *it looks like* . . .

'A hook!'

'Exactly,' said Sophie. 'And it just so happens that I know that a certain Father Thomas Hook, of Our Lady of the Silver Scales in Bankside, was a good friend of a certain Jacques Sauna-Lurker.'

The sound of footsteps was becoming audible, banging down the staircase, coming closer. Well, the sound wasn't coming closer. The sound waves were simply in the air, and indeed in Sophie and Robert's ears, and remained in place. But the feet that were making the sound were coming closer.

'Come on,' urged Sophie. 'Father Hook will be able to decipher the strange code. We've got to get to him!' She hauled him through the Fire Exit at the far end of the little hallway, and up a spiral staircase into the night.

4

The Exterminator stepped out into the clear night air. He had enjoyed himself at the brothel as only a man who had successfully completed an extermination can do. Now he had new tasks to complete, more vermin to be purged from the world, his near-sacred mission to be continued. He chuckled to himself as he strode down the street.

Always stay one step ahead of your foe, he thought to himself.

He walked up Blackfriars road towards Blackfriars bridge.

5

Robert and Sophie hurried up the Strand on foot, heading towards the location of the Church of Our Lady of the Silver Scales. Robert's head spun. Not literally spun, of course; not like that scene in *The Exorcist*, that would be just weird. And would suggest that he was possessed by the Devil. Which he wasn't. As far as I know. But his head span metaphorically. Only a couple of hours earlier he had been in his bed, blithely and peacefully slumbering! Since then he had been taken to the scene of an horrific murder, he had met a beautiful French woman, been accused of murder, and had fled the police.

'It's hard to take in,' he gasped, trying to keep up with Sophie Nudivue's powerful thighs. With the *strides taken* by Sophie Nudivue's powerful thighs, I mean. 'I can't believe that somebody is trying to frame me.'

'Somebody,' said Sophie. 'Or perhaps some *organisation*.'

'The deep conspiracy thing,' said Robert. 'Yes, you were telling me about that weren't you. Tell me . . . um, Miss Nudivue. Can I call you Sophie?'

'By all means.'

They passed Waterloo Bridge away to their right, and crossed the interchange into Fleet Street. To their left were the Royal Courts of Justice, home to the Court of Appeal, the High Court of Justice, and the Crown Court, all housed in a spectacular 1000-room Gothic mansion, designed and overseen by the great Victorian architect George Edmund Street, after whom several London Streets are named, amongst them George Edmund Street Street. Looking to his left, Robert could see the statues of Christ, King Solomon, King Alfred, and Moses, that are positioned above its main entrance.

'Sophie,' he asked. 'How did you know to come to the National Gallery just as I was being brought there?'

'I had an appointment to meet with Monsieur Sauna-Lurker this very evening,' she explained. 'At ten pm, in his office. I hoped to discuss with him certain aspects of a giant conspiracy that has begun to reveal itself to my investigation. Alas the conspiracy got to Sauna-Lurker first. They silenced him.'

'That doesn't explain how you knew that the police were about to arrest me.'

'Being attached to the Sûrité as I am,' said Sophie, airily, 'I have access to the London police radio bands, and so I heard about his murder, and also about the instructions to apprehend you – to pick you up from your Southwark apartment and transport you to the murder scene, only to arrest you there. But I knew as soon as I heard this that you were innocent! I have followed your work . . .'

'Have you?' said Robert, flattered. 'Really?'

'Indeed. More, I knew that the conspiracy would attempt to frame somebody. They would never risk being uncovered themselves. And when I heard your name . . .'

'It's jolly lucky for me that you did,' said Robert, earnestly. 'I mean jolly lucky.'

'Don't mention it.'

'No – really – it could be that today is my lucky day. In many ways.'

'Hmm.'

'Sophie,' said Robert, after a pause. 'Might I just ask? Are you . . . you know, seeing anybody at the moment? Are you single?'

'The church,' Sophie replied, with a rather studied nonchalance, 'is just up here . . .'

6

It was past ten o'clock by the time Robert and Sophie arrived at the Church of Our Lady of the Silver Scales, and slipped inside. 'This,' said Sophie, 'is the priest's church. We absolutely must speak to him – and we must speak to him right away. We cannot delay! The police have as good a chance of deciphering Sauna-Lurker's "hook" symbol as we had. Father Thomas Hook is well known as a cryptologist, and as a friend of Jacques Sauna-Lurker. They could be here any moment to question him themselves – or perhaps to take him into custody.'

'Right,' said Robert. 'And, just remind me, why are we talking to this chap?'

'Because he can decipher the strange message that Sauna-Lurker scrawled on the *Last Supper*!'

'Ah yes,' said Robert. He looked about him. 'So we've got to speak to the priest.'

'Yes, now—' Sophie urged. 'Go – find him.'

'Why me? Why don't you find him?'

'Because you are the expert with the codes. You can tell him what we know. You can ask him what Jacques meant by his strange message. Show him the sketch you made of it.'

'Right,' said Robert. 'Er – OK.' He looked about the dimly lit church, walking slowly down the aisle, which means 'wing' and is the name for the passage-ways that run down the sides of any given church, not, as many believe, for the central walkway. An elderly lady stepped from a large wooden box set against the wall of the building and started up the aisle towards the exit. 'Excuse me,' said Robert, politely. 'I am looking for Father Thomas Hook . . . do you know where he is?'

'He's taking confession right now,' said the old lady. She indicated the box from which she had just emerged.

'I see,' said Robert. 'In there?'

'That's right. Left hand door.' She walked off.

Sophie came over. 'Well,' she said. 'Go on – go in.'

'In there?' said Robert. 'I'm not going in there. I've never been in a confessional in my life. I wouldn't know how to start.'

'Start by saying "Forgive me father for I have sinned", and then tell Father Hook why we are here – impress upon him the importance of our speaking to him.'

'You do it.'

'No,' said Sophie. 'You.'

'Can't we,' said Robert, slightly querulously, 'wait until he comes out?'

'There's no time to waste!' insisted Sophie. She nudged him. 'Go on.'

Robert walked nervously over to the confessional and stepped inside. It was rather like a photo-booth except that it was made entirely from dark wood, and instead of a camera there was a wooden grill. And there was no slot for money, or any buttons, or any instruction panel telling you how to obtain a photograph. But I was hoping to suggest, rather, the overall scale of the confessional, and the fact that it had a little seat inside. Robert sat down.

Through the grill, Robert could see the shadowy silhouette of Father Hook.

'Forgive me father for I have sinned,' he said, just as Sophie had instructed him. Catholicism is a much more prevalent religious faith in France than in England, and it is not surprising that she knew the forms and rituals of the confessional.

'How long since your last confession?' the priest asked.

'How long?' said Robert, a little thrown. 'Long. Lengthy. Yes. Actually, the reason I'm here – I've got a little diagram.' He pulled out his notebook. 'I really need to talk to you about my little diagram.'

'We are talking, my son. Unburden yourself. What sins are troubling your conscience?'

'Sins? Right.' Robert hummed. 'Could we, maybe, talk about something else? I've a diagram I need to show—'

'Don't be shy, my son. Tell me of your sins.'

'But there are other things we need to talk about—'

'I am here,' said the priest, firmly, 'to hear confession of sins. Not idle chit chat.'

'Sins,' said Robert. 'Right. So, if I, um, tell you my sins, can we talk about something else after that?'

The priest paused, minutely. 'How do you mean, my son? "Something else?" You are seeking absolution from your sins, are you not? This is a confessional, after all.'

'But—'

'My son,' said the priest, more sternly. 'I sense that you are trying to avoid talking about what is on your conscience. You must confront it directly. I do not want to hear you prevaricate. I want to hear your sins.'

Robert resolved to confess to a sin, and when that was gotten out of the way to address the priest directly. 'OK,' he said. 'Well in terms of *sin*, I . . .

um . . .' But his mind was blank. He couldn't think of a single sin. He wracked his brain for the conventions of the Catholic faith. What he needed, he decided, was a relatively small sin, something to as it were *break the ice*, to open a channel of communication between himself and Father Hook. That would have to be a relatively minor sin, of course. He could hardly confess to – say – murder, and then hope to win the priest's trust afterwards. No: he needed a small, a venal, sin; a quick confession and then a proper conversation with the priest. But in the panic of the moment he could not think of a single one. He toyed with the notion of eating fish on a Friday. But was eating fish on Fridays a sin? Or was it *not* eating fish? He really couldn't remember.

'Sins,' said Robert, in a casting-about-a-bit sort of voice. 'Sins, sins.'

'My son,' said the priest. He sounded annoyed. 'Confession is a holy sacrament. You must not mock it. Either confess your sins to me, or I shall have to ask you to leave.'

'Could you give me a clue?' suggested Robert.

The priest's silence was not an encouraging silence. 'Clue?' he said, shortly. 'What do you mean, clue?'

'Well I was just wondering what my options might

be, sin-wise? I mean, if you could just, you know, give me a quick run-down, a top ten perhaps, then I could indicate which . . . um . . .'

'Have you never been to confession before, my son?' the priest asked sternly.

'Yes, yes, of course. Of course!' Robert tried a brief, carefree laugh, but it came out far from carefree. It sounded, instead, rather careful. Or care-y. 'Hah! Yes, of course I've been to confession before. Loads of times. It's just that, I mean, I've so *many* sins, it is hard to pick out just the one. Couldn't you just give me a general absolution for everything?' An idea popped into Robert's head. 'Yes, that's it. Tell you what, I confess to all of them.'

The priest was silent for a little while. 'All?' he repeated.

'Yes. I'm terribly sorry Father, I've committed all the sins. Can you absolute me? Absolve me, I mean? A blanket absolution should cover them. And once that's out of the way—'

'You are a soul in confusion,' said Father Hook gravely. 'Something has muddled your mind.'

'Hurry up!' hissed Sophie from the doorway of the confessional. 'Robert – hurry up. I think I can hear police sirens . . .'

Suddenly a sin popped into Robert's head. 'I've got

one,' he said excitedly, 'I've been coveting false idols. Will that do?'

There was a pregnant pause from the other side of the grill.

'You what?' asked the priest.

'Coveting them. There were these idols, you see, and the urge to covet them just came bubbling up inside me. I told myself, of course, come along Robert, be strong, resist the temptation to covet, but the lure of the thing, um, the idol, was too much for me.'

'Hurry *up*,' hissed Sophie, again. 'Have you shown him the diagram?'

'Father,' pressed Robert. 'Do I get absolution for the idols thing? Only I'm in something of a hurry.'

'Who *are* you?' barked the priest, angrily. 'What do you think you're *playing* at? And who is that prompting you from outside the confessional?' There was the sound of Father Hook getting up from his chair, and in a moment he had stepped out of the confessional. Robert assumed the confession was over.

He came out of the box back into the body of the church.

Father Hook was standing there, looking furiously at Sophie. 'You!' he cried. 'I told you to *stop bothering me*! Do you want me to call the police?'

'Father Hook,' said Sophie, pleadingly. 'You've got to listen to me . . . your life may be in danger . . .'

Hook turned to Robert. 'Are you in league with this delusional female?' he demanded.

The priest was an imposing figure; tall, broad-browed, raven-haired. Although, now I come to think of it, ravens don't have hair; they have feathers, everyone knows that. His wide face was dominated by a massy pyramidical nose, above which his two tiny, almost circular eyes clustered close together, as if competing with one another to alight at the apex, like the image of the Illuminatus's monument on the reverse of the American currency. He had a large black mole on his cheek of exactly the same colour as his large black cassock.

'You know her?' asked Robert.

'Indeed I do. An – excuse me mademoiselle, but I must speak the truth – an,' suddenly his voice swooped up in volume, rather like the Reverend Ian Paisley. Although, obviously, a Catholic Ian Paisley. If that isn't too impossible a notion to imagine – his voice swooped up in volume, 'an unspeakable filthy grubber-abouter! A miserable journalist feeding on the misery of others! A hack, hoping for a sensational headline, and with no more compassion than a stoat!'

'Father Hook,' pleaded Sophie, 'let me speak.'

'A journalist?' repeated Robert. 'She told me she was with the Sûrité!'

'A lie!' boomed the priest. 'She works for the *Crotte du Diable* – an execrable Parisian tabloid. She's been pestering me for months about some cranky crack-pot conspiracy kerfuffle.'

'I say,' said Robert brightly. 'That's good! That – I mean . . .' he went on, his smile flattening under the sour gaze of the priest '. . . that alliteration. I thought that was nice.'

'Entirely inadvertent,' he said. 'I have no idea whom you may be, sir, but if you are associating with this disreputable individual . . .'

'My name is Dr Robert Donglan,' said Dr Robert Donglan. 'I have just come from the scene of a terrible crime . . . Professor Jacques Sauna-Lurker, curator of the National Gallery . . . a friend of yours I believe?'

'Indeed he is,' declared Father Hook. 'A *good* friend.' His eyebrows dipped together minutely in suspicion. 'Do you know Jacques?'

'Alas no,' said Robert. 'He's dead.'

'Dead? No!' Father Hook actually reeled back in utter astonishment. His tiny circular eyes became even more perfectly circular. His mouth sagged open.

'I'm afraid so. Ms Nudivue and I have just come from the scene of the crime.'

'Father Hook,' said Sophie. 'I know we have had an . . . unfortunate series of encounters hitherto. But please believe me. The job with *Crotte* – that was merely a cover story. I am not actually a journalist. I am indeed, as I told Dr Donglan, a member of an elite group within the Sûrité. We have been investigating a number of conspiracies. The name *Eda Vinci* came up.'

If it was possible for the priest to look more astonished than he had done at hearing the news of Sauna-Lurker's death, he did so now. But in fact it was *not* possible for him to look more astonished, since his astonishment at the former news was so complete. So rather than doing the impossible thing of looking any more astonished, he continued looking astonished. 'How did you come by that name?' he demanded, in a low voice.

'Does it convince you that I am no mere hackette working on a lowly French tabloid?'

'It does,' said the priest. 'And poor Jacques dead? Incredible. Who is responsible for this crime?'

'That is a matter,' said Sophie, 'on which we hope you will be able to assist us.'

'You had better come into the Sacristy,' said the priest, indicating a door at the side of the church.

7

The Exterminator stood outside the Church. The façade was dominated by a silver-plated sculpture of the Virgin Mary, Mother of God, holding before her the scales of justice. The Exterminator chuckled to himself. Within this building, he reminded himself, a nest of vermin huddled in their lair, thinking themselves safe. But (he clutched his leather attaché-case to his chest) he possessed the necessary implements to ensure that they would never see another dawn.

His masters commanded it. The Exterminator had no intention of disobeying the direct command of his masters. The vermin – *qua* vermin – had it coming.

With an evil grin on his evil face, he stepped through the entrance and into the body of the church.

8

'I had to ask *you* to go into the confessional,' Sophie was explaining to Robert, as they sat in the Sacristy of the Church of Our Lady of the Silver Scales. 'I knew that Father Hook would recognise me, and reject what I had to say out of hand.'

'Well,' said the priest, reaching behind a pile of what Robert was sure he had described as vests to pull out a bottle of whisky, 'you have been making a veritable nuisance of yourself, Mademoiselle.' He unscrewed the bottle, poured whisky into the upended cap, and drank it down. This procedure he repeated six times in quick succession. 'I apologise, but I do not have any glasses. It would be quite inappropriate for me to keep whisky glasses in a Sacristy. A Sacristy is for sacred items of paraphernalia.' Seemingly refreshed, he recapped the bottle and stowed it away behind the pile of vests.

'I apologise if I have been nuisansical,' said Sophie. 'But you understand the deepness of this conspiracy, and the global implications of it . . .'

'Few understand that as well as I,' returned the priest. 'I have been researching the hidden secrets of this conspiracy for two decades. Jacques was my ally in this quest. For many years he and I have been getting closer and closer to the truth – Jacques even believed he had uncovered the true location of the Holy Grail.'

'The Holy Grail!' said Sophie. 'You don't say!'

'I do.'

'Did he tell you this location?'

'I'm afraid not.'

'How does the Holy Grail fit into this, exactly?' asked Robert. 'And who is this woman, this Eda Vinci you mentioned earlier?'

'I explained to you earlier, Robert,' said Sophie, 'that this conspiracy was a deep one, with many aspects. The Holy Grail is part of it. If Jacques knew the location of the most sacred and Holy Grail, then perhaps he was murdered to keep him quiet?'

'A lamentably effective strategy,' said the priest. 'For he can tell us nothing now that he is dead.'

'But perhaps he can!' Sophie said, eagerly. 'He left certain *clues* at the scene of his murder. One of them, written in blood on the hairdo of Christ, is this . . . Robert, show the Father your drawing of Jacques' message.'

Robert pulled out his notebook, flipped over the pages and held it up to Father Hook's gaze:

~~Baggels~~. Bagels.
Milk
Microwaveable Curry (<u>tikka</u>)
Eggs
Bacon
<u>Don't forget Clubcard</u>

'Oh hang on a mo,' said Robert, looking round at the page he was displaying. He flipped through a few more leaves, and then held up the sheet on which he had copied:

$$9 \ \Theta \ ? \ \circledcirc$$

The priest looked at this for a long while. 'No,' he said finally, scratching his mole. 'That doesn't mean anything at all to me.'

Sophie was crestfallen. Her crest fell at a rate of ten metres per second per second, which is the terminal velocity of any object dropped under the influence of Earth's gravitational pull. 'Are you sure? We believe that Jacques specifically indicated you as the one person who might be able to decipher this code.'

'Really?' said the priest. There was still a considerable residuum of suspicion in the way he regarded Sophie. 'Well it really doesn't mean anything to me.'

'I wonder,' said Robert, looking again at the code. 'I wonder if the last two symbols stand for "why-ay".'

Sophie Nudivue looked at him. 'What does that mean?'

'It doesn't really mean anything,' said Robert. 'It's just an expression people from the North East of England add to the ends of their sentences. But perhaps it means that Sauna-Lurker was indicating a Geordie?'

'What about the first two elements?'

'Nine somethings . . . I don't know.'

'There's only one person in London who could decipher this,' declared Father Hook, getting to his feet. 'Sir Herbert Teabag. One of Jacques' closest friends, and an expert in this sort of thing.'

'Do you know him?'

'My association with him has not been entirely friction-free,' said the priest sorrowfully. 'But the tragedy of Jacques death will surely enable us to overcome our petty differences.'

9

The priest owned a sports car, a detail which Robert found rather surprising. 'I often have to make house calls – administer the anointing of the sick, as extreme unction is now called, that sort of thing. This DB-7 is very handy for the London traffic.'

'I'm not complaining,' said Robert.

'Right, well let's all get in and . . . oh no!'

'What?'

'The keys!' The priest was looking horrified. 'I hang them on this little hook here – and now they're gone! Somebody has *stolen* them . . .'

'No!' cried Robert.

'It is almost,' said Sophie, horrified, 'as if some mysterious individual wishes to immobilise you, Father – to prevent you from leaving the church . . . to keep you here . . .' She looked with alarmed anticipation at the main entrance to the church . . .

10

'Ah, no,' said the priest in a more level tone of voice. 'Here they are, in my pocket all along. False alarm. Off we go . . .'

They all left the church and walked round the corner to where the nifty little car was parked. As soon as they had all got in, and pausing only to fasten his seatbelt, as is required by British law, Father Hook started the engine and drove off. 'It won't take us long,' he announced to his two passengers, sitting behind him. 'Teabag lives in Blackfriars; it's just over the river.'

'Who is this Teabag, exactly?' Sophie enquired.

'His full name is Herbert Alistair Teabag Bart.'

'But surely "Bart" is a first name, though,' observed Robert. 'Perhaps it should go between the Herb and the Al?'

'No,' explained the priest. ' "Bart" is short for "Baronet". It is a rank of English aristocracy, higher than a Knight but lower than a Baron. A Baron is a peer, entitled to sit in the House of Lords, for whom the proper mode of address is Lord so-and-so. Above a Baron in rank are, respectively, Viscount, Earl,

Marquess and Duke, then a royal Duke, and finally
Prince, Princess and King or Queen. A Baronet, such
as Sir Herbert, is not entitled to sit in the Lords, and is
addressed as "Sir" rather than "Lord".'

'And this Baronet is going to be able to help us, is
he? How, exactly?'

'He was one of Jacques Sauna-Lurker's oldest and
closest friends,' explained Father Hook, changing from
second to third gear and accelerating slightly as he
drove over London Bridge. 'They were in close cor-
respondence about what they called the Eda Vinci
mystery.'

'That name again!'

'Yes. Jacques and Teabag spoke on the phone often,
and Jacques was a frequent visitor to Sir Teabag's
London home – here.'

The car had pulled up outside an impressive if
bijoux townhouse in a quiet street not far north of
the river. The three travellers clambered from the car,
and made their way to the front door.

'Well, let's ring the bell.'

'A word of warning before we do,' said Father
Hook. 'I have had dealings with Sir Teabag before.
He suffers from an unfortunate nervous condition.'

'He's nervous?' asked Sophie.

'He's in good condition?' asked Robert.

'Perhaps both those things are true; but I meant instead that he suffers from what the psychiatric community calls *somatic tourette's syndrome*. In regular tourette's syndrome the sufferer is perfectly sane and rational, and yet cannot help shouting out obscenities. In Teabag's case the condition is much worse. He is a highly intelligent and lucid man mentally speaking; and yet he cannot control his body – he cannot help *lashing out* at people.'

'How unfortunate!' exclaimed Sophie.

'In a sense Teabag is lucky to be English. In some other countries sufferers from *somatic tourette's syndrome* are locked up in asylums. But acting eccentrically, even assaulting people unbidden, is part of the English national character. Nevertheless we must be careful. If one of his fits comes upon him . . .'

'I see,' said Robert.

'Furthermore, there has been something of a falling out between us,' said the priest. For many months Teabag, Jacques and I were working together trying to solve the mystery of Eda Vinci. But then Teabag became paranoid, convinced that I was a mole, that I had been placed there by the mafia-mason-illuminati nexus to assassinate him. That I was a creature of pure evil masquerading as a priest, a foul agent of wickedness.'

'And were you?' Robert queried. 'I mean, *are* you?'

'No,' said the priest.

'Right. And yet he suspected you?'

'He did.'

'Rather,' Sophie put in, smugly, 'as *you* suspected *me*, Father.'

There was a pregnant pause. Not, perhaps I should clarify, a pause that lasted nine months. That would be more than a pause, quite frankly. It would be more like a *hiatus*. Rather a pause that contained within it the possibility of something that would only later come to light. A pause that might make you sick in the mornings.

'Your point is taken,' said Hook, haughtily, looking down at her from behind his considerable *organon nasum*. 'I apologise for my misconception. Except that I only thought you were an opportunistic journalist, not an agent of the foulest conspiracy ever to have blighted the history of Europe. Anyway, the point is that Teabag may act strangely, and perhaps violently, even though his heart is in the right place. If he falls prey to one of his violent fits then the thing to do – this is how Jacques used to handle it – the thing to do is to restrain him. I happen to have some handcuffs about my person,' and he pulled the metal restraints from his cassock. 'We may need to use these.'

Donglan looked at the cuffs. 'You're sure that's the thing to do?'

'It will depend upon Sir Teabag, I'm afraid. You must trust me; I have had a great deal of experience with him. But don't worry; even if he has a fit and must be restrained, we'll probably still be able to communicate with him civilly. Even if he loses control of his *body*, and tries to attack us, he will still keep control of his *higher mental faculties*. That is the nature of *somatic tourette's syndrome*. In the past I've known him express genuine regret that he was trying to hit me with a poker even as he was trying to hit me with a poker.'

'What a strange notion!' said Robert.

'Enough talk,' said Sophie. 'Time is of the essence.'

'Essence-of-time,' agreed Robert. 'Yes. Let's ring the bell.'

They walked up the stone steps to Sir Herbert A. Teabag's black-painted front door. On the wood was hung a sign that read:

Public Order Notice
Beware of the Old English Eccentric.

This notice is required by magistrate's order.

Robert pushed the bell. It made a ding-dong-boing noise.

11

After a little while the door swung open to reveal Sir Herbert Teabag standing in his own hallway. Sir Teabag was a small man with a large head, rather in the fashion of those men and women in suits who impersonate Disney characters in Disneyland, although without their smiley natures, or desire to help visitors. His chinchilla-like body was clad entirely in tweed. His upper lip sported a walrus moustache; although unlike an actual walrus's Sir Herbert's moustache was composed of hair instead of thick tubular whiskers. He had a watery eye, a warty chin, a wary expression on his face, and a wry monocle wedged between his left cheek and left eyebrow.

'Yes?' he said, suspiciously, looking out at his three visitors. Then, recognising Father Hook, he added 'Garoo!' and tried to shut his visitors out.

But the priest had his foot in the door. Literally. And, now that I come to think of it, metaphorically too.

'Sir Herbert!' he bellowed, forcing his way in. Sir Herbert staggered backwards down the hall, and then took up a fighting stance near the bottom of his own stairs, which consisted of him standing with feet apart, arms forward, hands in 'karate' style. But there was something about this stance that made it only too obvious that Sir Teabag had no knowledge of karate at all.

'Wait for a minute, there, Sir Herbert,' called out Father Hook, holding his hands before himself placatingly. 'Just hold your horses. We've come just to talk – just to talk. Nothing more.'

'A likely story, Hook!' returned Teabag. 'Ya! Garoo!'

'It is indeed a likely story,' confirmed Hook, converting Teabag's ironic means-opposite-of-apparent-meaning phrase into a straightforward utterance of truth. 'This is Dr Robert Donglan from the University of London. And Sophie Nudivue, a researcher from the land of France. They are both researchers into . . . well, into *you know what*. And they are getting closer and closer to the truth. And I suggested to them that we come and speak to you. That's why we're here. We must talk . . . the events of earlier this evening. They possess a vital clue that only you might be able to decipher . . . a clue that could lead us to the true killers of Jacques.'

Teabag seemed to sag where he stood. The emotional blow of his friend's death was making itself visible upon him.

'Jacques . . .' he gasped.

'I'm afraid he is indeed dead,' said Hook, bleakly.

'Yes,' said Teabag, simply, lowering his karate-hands. 'I'd heard. I've only just got in. I've been out. But I saw on the *Eevny Stannit* news-stand that somebody has murdered Jacques inside his own Gallery . . .'

'It's too too true,' said, or perhaps stammered, Sophie. 'A terrible tragedy.'

'So you've been *out*, have you?' asked Father Hook, in a suspicious voice. 'Where did you go, might I ask? Anywhere near the National Gallery, eh? Eh?'

'I might,' bristled Teabag, 'ask *you* the same question, you — priest.' Robert was struck that this last word emerged almost as a term of abuse, even though it described Hook very precisely.

'How *dare* you impute,' said Hook, stepping forward, 'that I had something to do with dear Jacques death! He was my closest friend.'

'He was *my* closest friend, too!' retorted Teabag.

'Come, come, gentlemen,' put in Robert, trying to defuse the situation. 'He can't have been *both* of your closest friends, now can he?'

Everybody in the hallway looked at Robert.

'Why couldn't he?' said Sophie, shortly. 'What do you mean?'

'Think about it,' insisted Robert. ' "Closest" is an absolute term. Many things may be "close" or "closer" but only one might be "clos*est*". So when both Sir Herbert here *and* Father Hook claim that they were "closest" to the recently deceased, they can't both be right. Do you see?'

'Yes, I think I see the logical solecism here,' said Teabag, in a much less hysterical voice. 'The point is that Jacques might have been my closest friend from *my* point of view – and also have been this priest's closest friend from *his* point of view – without there being any contradiction in those two facts from *Jacques'* point of view.'

Robert thought about this for a while. 'I suppose you're right.' he said.

'Right. Good to have cleared that up. Where were we?'

'We were,' said Hook, 'accusing one another, by implication, of Jacques' murder.'

'So we were, so we were,' said Teabag, pleasantly. Then he yelled: 'How dare you! I loved Jacques like a brother – we *both* know that if anybody is likely to have killed him it will be the Catholic Church . . .'

A light went on in Robert Donglan's mind. *The Catholic Church.*

'Ah!' Robert said. 'Of course!' He tapped his own

forehead gently. '*That's* what the anagram was –
Chatholic Curch, *Catholic Church*! That's what he
wrote on the wall: that the *Catholic Church* had him
murdered!'

Teabag looked at Donglan. 'He wrote that on the
wall?'

'Yes,' said Donglan.

'That wasn't reported in the *Eevny Stannit.*'

'I don't believe it has been reported publicly. The
police took me to the murder scene, so I saw with my
own eyes. In fact,' he chuckled, 'they even accused me
of the crime! Fancy that!'

'But – but – they accused *you* – why?'

'Well, Sauna-Lurker had had this giant codfish
stuffed down his throat and apparently they found
my fingerprints on the fish. Obviously,' Robert said,
realising as he spoke how incriminating this must
sound to Teabag, and trying to throw a laugh into his
sentence to illustrate how risibly absurd it all was,
'*obviously*, somebody was trying to frame me for the
murder. Obviously.'

Teabag's eyes had assumed a rather wild shimmer.
'You!' he gasped. 'You're in it together! You're all in
it together! You all murdered Jacques together, and
now you've come to murder me! Help! Help!'

'His grief at Jacques' death has unhinged him,'

Father Hook said to Robert and Sophie *sotto voce*, which is to say, in Italian, 'in a small voice'. Not that he spoke to them in Italian, which Robert and possibly Sophie would not have understood. It's just that that is the phrase one uses to indicate that a speaker is speaking in a small voice. I don't know why there isn't an equivalent English phrase. Perhaps a suitable English translation might be 'in a voice like Sooty's'. 'Let's cuff him, and try to calm him down.'

'Nobody wants to murder you,' said Sophie, holding her hands in front of her and advancing on the Baronet.

'Herbert, we have known one another for years,' said Hook in a soothing voice. 'You must trust us! We are trying to discover who Jacques' murderer is. That's why we've come here – you may be able to help us.'

Teabag looked wildly from face to face and then, bizarrely, his whole manner changed. A calmness took hold of his features, and he spoke in a level voice. 'Of course,' he said. 'I apologise for my over-reaction. It was a terrible shock to hear of poor Jacques' demise. Why don't we go through to my study and have a drink, talk about what to do next? A little drink, Hook? Would you like?'

Hook beamed. 'That's more like it, my dear

fellow,' he said. 'I must say I was a little worried that you—'

There were two sounds simultaneously. One was a sort of *thwok* noise, such as might be made by hitting a watermelon with a sock full of coins. The other was a voice saying, with excessive loudness, 'Would you like a *snifter*, priest? Eh? Eh?' The latter sound, Robert realised, was coming from Teabag's mouth; he had leaped forward and coshed Hook over the head with a wooden carved owl that he had grabbed from a shelf. For the briefest moment Donglan was stunned by the disparity between Teabag's words – politely offering his guest a drink – and the irrational violence of his actions. Then he understood.

'He's having one of his fits,' he called to Sophie. 'His body is beyond the control of his conscious mind! We must restrain him!'

But Mademoiselle Nudivue was way ahead of him. She rushed to the fallen figure of the priest, picked up the cuffs, and turned on Teabag.

Once again the Baronet demonstrated a strange disparity between his spoken words and his actions. His mouth was saying 'I have no desire to injure a lady!' but his body was swiping at her with the carved owl, in clear contradiction of his words.

'Sophie!' called Robert, in an agony of anticipation. 'Be careful!'

But Sophie was more than a match for the elderly British aristocrat. In a single graceful movement she ducked under his outstretched arm, knocked the owl from his hand, grabbed his elbows and pressed them together behind his back. Indeed, although she was smaller and slenderer than Teabag, she displayed a surprising strength of muscle. In a trice the handcuffs were on Teabag's wrists, looped through the pole at the bottom of the stair banisters and, struggle as he might, he was restrained.

12

Sophie went straight to the supine body of the priest, where Robert joined her. 'He's out cold,' she said, moving him into the recovery position. 'Still breathing, but unconscious.'

'Oh I *do* hope I haven't hurt him,' said Teabag, although he was hopping and wriggling and trying to get free of the handcuffs even as he spoke these words of remorse.

'We'd better phone for an ambulance,' said Robert.

'This is a terrible development,' Sophie deprecated. 'Phoning for an ambulance will be tantamount to alerting the police that we are here. We will have to leave – and yet we are no closer to discovering the terrible secret for which Jacques was murdered.'

'Perhaps Sir Herbert will still help us,' said Robert.

Sophie looked up at him, chained to the banister with his arms behind him, wriggling and shaking in rage and terror, and said 'do you really think so?'

'Remember what Father Hook told us. This is one of those fits of madness of which he spoke. Although his body has violently lost control, his mind is clear and sane. Hook's account of *somatic tourette's syndrome* describes these symptoms to a "t". And indeed to a "b", an "a" and a "g".'

'You've chained me to the banisters!' Teabag cried, struggling. 'You came into my house with handcuffs and chained me to the banisters!'

'You see?' said Robert. 'That's a straightforward statement of fact; the mark of a rational and therefore sane mind.'

'Well I suppose so,' said Sophie, dubiously.

'Call an ambulance!' Teabag cried.

Robert looked over at the phone in the hallway. 'Look,' he said. 'The little blinking light is flashing; what does that mean?'

Sir Teabag had stopped struggling, and seemed to have slumped into a state of resignation. 'That's the answerphone,' he said in a low voice. 'Press the little green button.'

Robert, glad to hear the baronet sounding less fitty, did as he was instructed. There was a beep, and a mechanical voice declared: 'You have one new message. Message, today, at seven twenty-eight pm . . .'

Then the hall was filled with the sound of coughing:

Co-u-gh! cof! co-u-gh! cof! co-u-gh! co-u-gh! co-u-gh! co-u-gh! cof-cof!

'Jacques!' cried Teabag, starting to struggle against his restraints once again. 'That's the sound of Jacques' coughing . . . I'd recognise that anywhere! My poor Jacques – murdered! Let me go you two – release me – undo me!'

'Come now, Sir Herbert,' said Sophie. 'Your mind may be rational, but your body is beyond your conscious control. You know we cannot release you.'

Robert was pondering the phone message. 'He rang up to *cough* at you?' he said, puzzled. 'Just that? Why would he do that?'

'He was an inveterate smoker,' said Sophie. 'He was famous for it.'

'An invertebrate smoker?' gasped Robert, surprised.

'Inveterate,' corrected Sophie. 'But don't you see what this means? This message was left at seven twenty-eight pm! That's immediately before he was murdered!'

'Murderers!' yelled Teabag, confirming Sophie's statement with such volume that it was almost as if he hoped to be audible to people in the street outside. 'Break-in! Violence! Murder!' he was still struggling violently. Robert marvelled that so thorough-going a physical seizure could nevertheless leave Teabag's mind sane enough to summarise the events at the National Gallery so pithily.

'But why would Jacques ring Sir Herbert only to cough at him?' Sophie asked.

'Perhaps he *couldn't* speak. Perhaps the cod was already down his throat.'

'He could hardly cough with a cod down his throat. No, this must have been before the murder.'

'You mean . . . ?'

'I'm assuming he had already encountered the assassin, and perhaps had struggled with him. Maybe the assassin had already cut those slashes on either side of his neck. But it must have been before the codfish was actually stuffed into his throat. So he *could* have spoken, but chose not to.'

'Well, perhaps he didn't want to speak because the murderer was in the room with him.'

'So he coughed to convey a message without the murderer understanding?' said Sophie. 'Brilliant! But what was he saying?'

'How many *times* did he cough?' asked Robert. 'Perhaps it is some kind of code. Perhaps a coughing version of morse code. What do you think, Sir Herbert?'

'Four cough!' yelled Sir Teabag, excitedly. 'Let me go! Use odds! Four cough!' He wriggled and danced.

'Four? No there were certainly more than four,' said Robert. 'I counted at least ten.'

'Let me *go*!'

'That's still barely enough elements for a message in morse code,' said Sophie. 'Many morse code letters require three components, like dot-dot-dot. Some even require more than three.'

'Yes,' said Robert. 'So a mere ten elements might be conveying as few as three letters.'

'Three letters,' mused Sophie.

'Not so much morse code as *less* code,' said Robert, and grinned. Sophie seemed oddly unmoved by the joke. 'It's a joke,' he explained, thinking perhaps that his humour had not translated from English into her French mind. 'Do you see? Do you get it?' He turned to the Baronet. 'You get it, don't you, Sir Teabag?'

'Four cough!' shouted Sir Teabag again, struggling against his handcuffs.

'No it was certainly ten,' said Robert. 'But the question is: what message is being *communicated* by the coughs?'

'Go boil your heads!'

'No,' said Sophie. 'That would have required many more than ten dots and dashes.'

'Drop dead!' yelled the Baronet.

'He did indeed drop dead,' agreed Robert, soberly. 'And we owe it to his memory to decipher his last message to us.'

'If the softer, throat-clearing coughs stand in for *dots*,' Sophie suggested, 'and the louder phlegm-shunting chesty coughs for *dashes* . . .'

'Of course!' barked Robert. 'By George, I think you've got it. Now, hang on a mo, I happen to have a card in my wallet that gives the morse code equivalents for the letters of the alphabet.' He rummaged around in his pocket. 'Here you go.'

A	·-	N	-·
B	-···	O	---
C	-··-·	P	·--·
D	-··	Q	--·-
E	·	R	·-·
F	··-·	S	···
G	--·	T	-
H	····	U	··-
I	··	V	···-
J	·---	W	·--
K	-·-	X	-··-
L	·-··	Y	-·--
M	--	Z	--··

'Play the recording again,' suggested Sophie.

Robert pressed the button on the answerphone, and Sauna-Lurker's voice was once again audible:

Co-u-gh! cof! co-u-gh! cof! . . . Co-u-gh! co-u-gh!
co-u-gh! . . . Co-u-gh! cof-cof!

'Right,' said Robert, consulting the chart. 'Well, *long-short-long-short* is "C" . . .'

'Yes,' agreed Sophie, looking over his shoulder. 'And *long-long-long* is "O".'

'Well everybody knows "O" in morse,' said Robert, smugly. 'That's the middle letter of SOS, isn't it. *Everyone* knows that.'

'And *long short-short* is "D".'

'There you have it. COD.' Robert looked pleased with himself. Then he frowned. 'His own murder weapon? He didn't need to tell us that he was about to be murdered with a cod . . . and certainly not in such an oblique, roundabout manner. That doesn't make any sense. Why would a dying man bother to cough C-O-D? Why couldn't he just *say* it?'

'But how do we know if we're hearing the pauses between letters in the right places? What if the first letter is long-short-long-short-*long*? That's "K". Then long-long-long, "O", and short-short, which is "I".'

'KOI?' queried Robert. 'What's that?'

'It's a kind of carp.'

'So,' said Robert, meditatively. 'It could be either COD or CARP. Both types of *fish*.'

'Oh very different sorts of fish,' said Sophie, with a dismissive shake of her head. 'Cod belongs to the family *Paracanthopterygii*, which includes toadfish, trout and perch as well as cod. Carp belongs to a wholly different family, the *Ostariophysi*, which includes nearly six thousand different varieties of carp, minnows, loaches and catfish.'

Robert stared at her for a moment in frank admiration, and indeed physical desire. 'That's amazing! How do you know so much about fish?'

'Just one of those things that I've picked up,' she said, blushing. 'During my busy and adventurous life.'

She blushed extremely attractively. Robert found himself wishing he could do something to summon that blush to her cheek – something embarrassing, or insulting perhaps. But, he reminded himself, now is not the time for romantic speculation. Perhaps later . . .

'It doesn't get us any closer to solving the mystery', he said.

'Presumably Monsieur Sauna-Lurker wanted to say cod *to us* in such a way that the murderer, even though he was overhearing him, would not understand,' said Sophie.

Robert patted Sophie's shoulder. 'Please don't take this the wrong way,' he said, in what he hoped was a letting-her-down-gently voice, 'and in general I'd say your command of and fluency in spoken English is excellent. But the English word is "*Mister*", not "*Monsieur*".'

Sophie glowered at him. 'I know that.'

'Well,' said Robert, beaming at her, 'I'm only saying. If nobody corrects your English then you're never going to improve. The point is that it would be more correct to say "Mister Sauna-Lurker". That's all I'm saying.'

'You really think I don't know the English word "*Mister*"?' fumed Sophie. 'What kind of fool do you take me for?'

'A very attractive and alluring fool,' purred Robert. He reconsidered what he had just said, and decided that perhaps it did not create the impression he was hoping to create. It had sounded, in his head, before he spoke the words, witty and disarming. But somehow it had come out of his mouth as rather patronising and even insulting. 'So, yes, well, by which I *mean to say*,' he added, in what he hoped was a smooth recovery, 'that I don't consider you a fool at all. You're not a fool. You are the opposite of a fool, whatever that is. A wise man. That's the sort of way I look at you. So, to reiterate, nothing foolish about you. Although the attractive and alluring part still holds. And . . . um . . . when I said wise man back there I wasn't trying to suggest that you look like a man. And especially not like a man with a long beard and a camel, ha-ha-ha!' But his laughter sounded unusually forced. 'I seem,' he continued, in a graver tone of voice, 'to have tied myself rather into knots! What I've been trying to say is that . . . well, look there's been something I've been meaning to ask you, Sophie. Fate seems to have thrown us together; but I can't believe I am mistaken in sensing a certain – what's the French word? Help me out here . . . a certain *rappaport*.'

'*Rapport*,' corrected Sophie, icily.

'Yes. That. Or – what did I say?'

'You spoke the name of your country's most famous dwarf actor.'

'Did I? Did I really? Well that's very interesting. But not really relevant. Because what I want to say to you isn't dwarfish in any sense. Not that's there's anything wrong with being a dwarf. Indeed, I understand that it's not especially polite to refer to dwarves as dwarves any more. We're supposed to say persons of restricted height. Although that's by-the-by. The point is,' Robert continued, growing more and more nervous the longer he went on, 'is that I've been thinking about this for a long time, that on the basis of our rappaport . . . well, I want to ask *you*, how would you like to go out with me? We could start by

planning a meal together, in a nice restaurant somewhere, and take it from there? What do you say?'

Sophie stared levelly at him. 'Dash-dot, dash-dash-
dash,' she said.

13

The Baronet's physical seizure seemed to have abated a little. He had slid the chain down the banister pole and was now sitting on the foot of the stairs looking glum. Robert assumed his expression reflected his grief at the death of his friend.

'Sir Herbert?' Robert enquired. 'Do you know why Sauna-Lurker left you that particular message?'

'He was my friend,' Teabag replied, in a miserable voice.

'Yes, yes,' said Robert impatiently. 'But we really haven't time for that now. We must decipher the clues! Why would he cough COD at you?'

'Will you please release me?' Teabag pleaded, tears in his eyes. 'In my own home! To barge in here, assault me, chain me to my own banisters . . .'

'But look what you did to Father Hook!' Sophie pointed out. 'He's out cold.'

'He was coming to murder me,' said Teabag. 'Just as he murdered Jacques.'

Robert made to express his disbelief by saying 'pshaw!' It was the kind of thing he often read in books, and liked the look of it, and he had in fact been waiting for a good opportunity to try it out in real life. This was the perfect occasion. 'pshaw!' he said, shaking his head. Unfortunately, on account of his lack of practice with the expression, his 'pshaw!' came out as 'P. Shaw', and that sounded like a name.

Both Teabag and Sophie looked at him.

'But what I don't understand,' said Sophie, turning back to the Baronet, 'is why you're so convinced Father Hook wanted to murder you?'

'Who's this P. Shaw?' Teabag inquired.

'I'm sorry,' said Robert. 'That came out wrong, actually. I didn't mean to say that.'

'Never mind that now,' Sophie pressed. 'Tell me why you're so convinced Father Hook wanted to marry you?'

'Marry me?'

'Not marry – murder.'

'But,' Teabag pointed out, 'you said marry.'

'Did I?' said Sophie. 'Really? That must have been a Freudian slip. I meant murder.'

'Ah,' said Robert. 'A Freudian slip, really? One of those occasions, identified by the great Austrian psychotherapist Sigmund Freud, who as we all know was born in 1856 in Vienna and died in 1939 in London, when the subconscious mind subtly changes what we intended to say, replacing the word with one that carries some significant emotional cathexis from our Id?'

'Yes,' said Teabag, 'one of those.'

'That's a very *interesting*, slip, I think,' Robert opined. 'To switch "murder" and "marry" like that. Very significant, I'd say.'

Sophie stamped her foot. 'Enough! We don't have time for these games! Tell me, Sir Herbert, *why are you so convinced Father Hook wanted to murder you?*'

Teabag looked sulkily at the floor, and dragged his handcuff chain up and down the banister pole. 'The Catholic Church,' he muttered. 'They will stop at nothing to silence our research. We are on the verge of uncovering the greatest mystery of the last two thousand years – one that will rock the Catholic Church to its very foundations. Naturally they aim to stop us . . . by any means necessary.'

'But . . . murder?' whispered Robert, horrified. 'Murder is, like, really really nasty. It might even be a sin. In fact, the more I think about it, the more convinced I become that it is indeed a sin.'

'You think they care about *that* when their very existence is under threat?'

'But why *cod*?' Sophie demanded. 'I don't see how that fits into the picture.'

'Jacques and I had been discussing a . . . certain

picture,' said Teabag. 'He claimed, after a great deal of research and hard bargaining, to have obtained this picture, and to have secreted it about his gallery.'

'The *Mona Eda* . . .' gasped Sophie.

That made Teabag look up. 'What do you know about that? How can you possibly know about that?'

'Because I've been on the same trail, Sir Herbert!' Sophie gushed. 'The *Mona Eda* has been my life's work!'

'I thought that only Jacques and I knew . . .' Herbert rasped. He seemed overcome with emotion.

'So the picture is in the National Gallery?' said Sophie, tremendously excited. 'It's there – right now?'

'I wasn't sure,' said Teabag. 'Jacques was supposed to telephone me tonight, to let me know whether he'd been able to smuggle it into his gallery. Instead of which he was murdered.' Teabag slumped again.

'But not before he conveyed to you his final message,' Sophie reminded him. '*Cod*. Why did he cough *cod* at you?'

'I don't know,' said Teabag miserably. 'I've really no idea.'

'Doesn't it mean anything to you?'

'Nothing at all.'

'I suppose,' Robert put in, trying to be helpful, 'that he didn't have time to cough out The Picture Has Successfully Been Smuggled Into The Gallery. I mean,'

he added, fishing out his chest-card, 'that would have
been like—' and he started coughing:

> *Co-u-gh! . . . Cof-cof-cof-cof! . . . Cof! . . . Cof!*
> *co-u-gh! co-u-gh! cof! . . . Cof-cof! . . . Co-u-gh!*
> *cof! co-u-gh! cof! . . .*

Sophie ignored him. 'It must mean *something*,' she said
to Teabag. 'You were expecting a phone call from
Jacques confirming or denying whether he had been
able to obtain . . .' she couldn't stop herself from
shaking her head in frank disbelief and amazement,
'. . . actually *getting his hands* on the original *Mona Eda*?'

'I was,' said Sir Teabag, hanging his head in misery.

'Well, if we assume that he couldn't say those
words directly because the assassin was in the room
with him, and we assume that he knew the assassin
would snatch the phone from his hand, so that he
wouldn't have much time . . .'

In the background, Robert was still coughing:
'. . . *Cof-cof! . . . Co-u-gh! cof! . . . Co-u-gh! . . .*
Cof-cof-cof-cof! . . . Cof! . . .'

'Then,' Sophie concluded, 'that one word he *did*
communicate *must* mean something. Think! He intended it for your ears . . . cod. Cod, Sir Teabag!
Think! Cod! Cod! Think! Cod! Think!'

'But it conveys nothing to me!' exclaimed the Baronet in an agonised tone of voice. 'Apart from . . .'

'Apart from . . .'

'. . . *Cof!* . . . *Cof! co-u-gh! cof!* . . . *Co-u-gh! cof! co-u-gh! co-u-gh!*' concluded Robert, and put away his cheat sheet. 'Which,' he added, in a raspy voice, 'would obviously have taken too long.' He made a noise like a cat with furballs. 'Arrhh!' he whispered, hoarsely. 'I seem to have scraped my throat rather doing that.'

'COD,' barked Sophie.

'The only thing it *can* mean,' said Sir Herbert '. . . but if you know about the *Mona Eda*, then you must know about that as well.'

'You mean . . . ?'

'Yes, the C.O.D. itself . . . the *Conspiratus Opi Dei*.'

'No!' gasped Sophie.

'Yes,' confirmed Sir Herbert.

'You what?' queried Robert.

'It's more a legend than a fact . . .' Sophie explained. 'The conspiracy behind all conspiracies. *Conspiratus Opi Dei*. The Conspiracy of the Work of God. The Catholic Church is merely one of several front organisations for this shadowy, ancient, gathering. You see, conspiracy, in the original Latin, meant first of all a *breathing together*, a coming together of souls. Only later did it acquire its negative connotations of a secret cabal plotting for malign purposes.'

'The entire Catholic Church is merely a front organisation for this particular conspiracy?' boggled Robert. 'That's quite an allegation.'

'Not *just* the Catholic Church,' said Teabag in a low voice. '*All* the conspiracies of the world are masks deliberately worn by the C.O.D. to hide their very existence. Whilst people are busy chasing after the Illuminati, or the Masons, or the Mafia, they are distracted from the *real* secret power of this world.'

'The Mafia?' said Robert. 'Are they part of it too?'

'A deeply spiritual organisation, an ancient branch of the Catholic Church,' confirmed Sophie. 'It used to be well known, although now the Mafia has done a very good job of covering up its origins.'

'The *Mafia*?' repeated Robert, incredulously. 'Are you sure? I've never heard that they were a spiritual branch of any church . . . aren't they more like, you know, Italians in expensive suits shooting people and doing this gesture' – he put all the fingers'-ends of his right hand together, facing up, and waggled the hand back and forth – 'a lot? That's the Mafia, right? Organised crime?'

'But you see that's *exactly* what I'm talking about, that kind of preconception,' said Sophie. 'You've no actual experience of the Mafia. All you know comes through *The Godfather* and *The Sopranos*. But those representations are designed deliberately to mislead you. The reality is very different. Do you know where the name *mafia* comes from? Do you know what it means?'

'I heard it was an acronym for Mothers And Fathers of Italian American origin,' said Robert.

Sir Teabag made a scoffing noise. 'That would be Mafoiao' he pointed out. 'Which is quite hard to say.'

'Mafia,' said Sophie, 'means *my faith* – ma-fia. It's a *spiritual* designation, associated from its earliest days with the Papacy and the Catholic Church. But that's only to say that it is a manifestation of a deeper secret organisation. They have tentacles everywhere – in Hollywood, where the *Godfather* films were made. In N.A.S.A., where the moon landings were faked. Here in Britain, where the Royal Family are run as a complex scam.'

'You mean the Royal Family really are lizards?'

'Lizards? No. Not lizards. But they are part of a more ancient bloodline than any English aristocracy

. . . and the lizard theory is not a million miles away from the truth.'

'This is incredible!'

'It's so obvious!' exclaimed Sophie excitedly. 'Of course . . . this explains everything! The C.O.D. are behind the murder of Jacques Sauna-Lurker.'

'I fear you are correct,' said Sir Herbert. 'Jacques had somehow obtained the original *Mona Eda*. The *Conspiratus* found out about it, and murdered him before he could reveal it to the world.'

'They would certainly have the power to infiltrate the National Gallery.'

'What about framing me?' put in Robert. 'Would they have the power to do that?'

'They would indeed,' said Sophie. 'They control most of the big Computing Companies, as well as most of the Companies engaged in research on genetic engineering. It would have been a relatively simple matter for them to have obtained your fingerprint, Robert – then genetically modify a codfish so that each of its scales reproduced your fingerprint in its dermal papilla, such that it came into relief in the scale enamel in the fully developed fish. Then they could take the fully grown fish and use it as a murder weapon . . . thereby implicating you in the murder.'

'But why *me*?'

'Perhaps they wanted to kill two birds with one stone. Perhaps you had been getting too close to them in your researches?'

'Yeah,' said Robert. 'Right.'

'It hardly matters whom they frame,' said Teabag. 'The only important thing for them is that they deflected attention away from themselves. If the murder were investigated too deeply then perhaps a ray of light might be cast into the gloom in which they hide . . . much better to give the police apparently watertight evidence that Dr Robert Donglan was the killer.'

'Watertight!' said Robert, grinning. 'I like that!' His two companions looked blankly at him. 'You know – fish scales. Watertight. Oh,' he added, in a lower voice. 'I thought you were making a joke.'

'Hardly,' said Sir Teabag. 'My best friend has been murdered. This really isn't a time to crack jokes.'

'Oh,' said Robert. 'No, I see. Quite.'

'Jacques Sauna-Lurker is dead,' Sophie said. 'But perhaps the *Mona Eda* is still in the Gallery. It may not be too late.'

'The assassin – whomsoever he is – will surely have removed the incriminating picture from the gallery,' said Teabag, shaking his head.

'Perhaps – but *perhaps not*! What if Jacques had

hidden the picture? Hidden it so well that the assassin couldn't find it?'

'But if *he* couldn't find it, then what makes you think *we* will be able to?' asked Sir Herbert.

'We have what the assassin didn't have,' said Sophie triumphantly. 'We have Jacques' last word. We have *COD*!'

'You think it is more than merely Jacques' way of identifying his killer?' asked Teabag. 'You think it might be a clue as to the hiding place of the *Mona Eda* within the National Gallery?'

'Yes.'

'*Mona Eda*?' asked Robert, with an expression on his face rather like a lost dog contemplating a sign-post. 'You keep going on about it. What is it, exactly?'

'There's no time to explain it to you now, Robert,' said Sophie. 'I'll tell you all about it on the way to the Gallery.'

'We're going to the Gallery?'

'With all speed. We have to see whether the picture is there or not.'

'But it's two in the morning!'

'We'll have to find a way in – break in, if necessary.'

'Wait!' cried Sir Teabag. 'What about me? You can't leave me here.'

Sophie looked long and hard at the Baronet. 'If we uncuff you, you have to promise not to attack us.'

'I promise.'

'Can we take the risk?' worried Robert. 'I mean – look what he did to Father Hook.' Everybody looked down at the supine figure of the priest. His breathing was audible. Indeed it sounded rather like snoring.

'But I thought you were assaulting me,' said Teabag, mildly. 'I was only defending myself.'

'Ah,' said Robert, pointing out the flaw in the Baronet's logic, 'but we *weren't* attacking you. Do you see? Do you see where you went wrong?'

'Well I see that *now*. But I had just learned that my best friend had been murdered – because he had gotten close to the secret of the C.O.D. And I too have also gotten close to that secret. And I knew that they knew, that the C.O.D. knew, and moreover that they knew that I knew. Which they also knew. I was expecting an assassination attempt. You can understand why I was jumpy.'

'OK,' said Robert, a little dubiously.

'Besides,' Teabag went on, 'I'm still not entirely sure about Hook. How well do either of you know him? How do you know you can trust him? He *is* a priest after all.'

'Not all the members of the Catholic Church are

members of the *Conspiratus*,' Sophie pointed out. 'In fact, only a small elite are even aware of the existence of the C.O.D. I'm sure Hook is innocent.'

'It's immaterial now,' said Teabag. 'He's out cold.'

'I'd better phone for that ambulance,' said Robert.

14

After they had called for an ambulance, and uncuffed Sir Teabag, they all got into Father Hook's sports car to hurry back to the National Gallery, having previously prised the car keys from the unconscious priest's trouser pocket. They then dragged his body out onto the front step, so that the medics could reach him; after which Sir Teabag locked his house. 'Can't be too careful,' he said. 'Burglars and all.' He looked down at the unconscious body of his friend. 'I do hope poor old Hooky's head isn't too sore when he wakes up,' he said.

Teabag drove, whilst Sophie and Robert sat in the back seat together. 'So,' said Robert, using the occasion to squeeze a little closer to the attractive French woman sitting beside him. 'You were saying something about a *Mona Eda*?'

'It's been a chimera for researchers into conspiracy,' said Sophie.

'Well, right,' said Robert. 'That doesn't tell me very much, partly because I don't know what a chimera is.'

'The word *chimera* derives from the Greek χιμαιρα,'

Sophie explained, 'which originally referred to a fabulous monster from ancient Lycia that vomited fire and was made up of the front part of a lion, the middle part of a goat and the hinder parts of a dragon. But since this creature patently never existed, "chimera" in common English usage came to mean any imaginary monster comprised of incongruous parts, and then later to mean any illusion, fabrication or especially any unrealisable or unrealised dream or quest-object. It was in this latter sense that I was using the term.'

'I see,' said Robert, shortly.

'Various specialists have postulated the existence of the *Mona Eda*. But now it seems as if we have the first concrete lead.'

'Concrete?' queried Robert, 'Lead? That's a pretty weighty combination.'

'Not "led",' corrected Sophie, annoyed that her slight French accent had misled her interlocutor, ' "Leed" '.

'Ah. So what is it, exactly, this *Mona Eda*? Some sort of picture, you were implying?'

'Have you heard,' said Sophie by way of replying, looking out of the window of the speeding car, 'of Leonardo?'

'Da Vinci? Of course.'

'Leonardo is world famous, of course. But there is

one thing that is little known about him – that in fact is only now being unearthed by scholars – that he was not an only child. In fact his mother had twins: the boy Leonardo, and a girl called *Eda*. They grew up together, and were very close, and yet whilst everybody has heard of Leonardo only a very few specialists have heard of the sister, Eda.'

'But why?'

'In part that's just a reflection of the age in which she lived, a world ruled by men, in which women – even brilliant women – never got the chance to achieve their potential. Like Shakespeare's sister – you've heard of Shakespeare's sister?'

Robert paused before replying, 'The pop group?'

Sophie ignored this. 'Renaissance Italy was a patriarchal culture. It valued men, and thought of women only as chattel. Women were for marriage, for childbirth and for domestic chores. It's hardly surprising that Eda, though a brilliant artist in her own right, never got the chance to work professionally.'

After a short pause Sophie continued, her words freighted with some buried emotional significance. 'People think of Leonardo as an outsider,' she said, 'as somebody ignored and unrecognised by his own age; but that description fits Eda much better. Leonardo was one of the most successful artists of his day;

he was apprenticed to Andrea del Verrocchio's studio, which Eda never was. He was given commissions by the Florentine authorities; he worked for Lorenzo de Medici, the most powerful man of his age; and for Lodovico Sforza, another very powerful figure. He knew the Pope personally. Eda had none of these advantages. Indeed, it seems that she couldn't even afford to buy the most basic artists' materials, and had to beg offcuts of canvas and bits and pieces from her brother when *she* wanted to paint.'

'So she was a painter too?'

'A great painter. A better painter, arguably, even than Leonardo. It's a lamentably common occurrence in European history that a brilliant artist or poet owes his fame to his gender, and that an even more brilliant female is ignored by posterity. Do you know about Dorothy Wordsworth?'

Robert decided this was a trick question. 'Do I know what about Dorothy Wordsworth? I mean, which of the many interesting things that I know about Dorothy Wordsworth are you interested in . . . ?'

'William Wordsworth remains perhaps the most famous English Romantic poet. He wrote a great many poems in the first half of the nineteenth-century. Perhaps you've heard his poem "Daffodils"? "I wandered lonely as a cloud that floats on high o'er vale and hill?" '

'Yes!' said Robert, delighted finally to recognise something.

'Well Dorothy wrote that.'

'But you just said *William* Wordsworth wrote it . . .'

'That's right. William published the poem under his own name and took all the credit. But he stole it from Dorothy. She kept a journal, and wrote down all her observations about the natural world. William read it, took out the most striking images and thoughts and published them as his own.'

'Brothers!' tutted Robert. 'That's so typical. I remember once when my little sister was only six, she had this Cindy doll, and I . . .'

'The case of Wordsworth,' said Sophie firmly, 'is quite well known amongst academics and students. What is not so well known is that many of *Leonardo's* most famous images are reworkings of original art produced, first of all, by Eda – by his sister.'

'I see.'

'The official explanation for the neglect of Eda's work,' Sophie continued, 'is similar to the explanation for Dorothy Wordsworth's relative neglect: the in-grained sexism of European culture, a society only interested in great *men* not great women. But I have long suspected that this is not the real reason. Eda's work has been much more comprehensively suppressed than Dorothy Wordsworth's. Nobody burned Dorothy's journals, for instance.'

'Did they *burn* Eda's pictures, then?'

'That was what was thought, for a long time. Certainly almost all the records of Eda's very existence have been expunged from official Florentine and Milanese records of the period. It seemed an impossible dream to recover any of her artwork. But I believe that is what Jacques Sauna-Lurker managed to do . . . and perhaps this is why he was murdered!'

'To preserve the reputation of Leonardo?' boggled Robert. 'That hardly sounds a likely motive for murder!'

'There's more to it than that,' said Sophie. 'I believe that Eda's art contained certain . . . clues . . . certain elements that Leonardo omitted when he copied his sister's paintings in order to sell them on to wealthy patrons.'

'How do you mean, clues?'

'Well that's the six million euro question. If we knew that, then perhaps we'd be able to get to the bottom of this whole mystery. My hypothesis is that Eda belonged to the *Conspiratus Opi Dei* herself. She may have placed certain clues as to the core mysteries of that organisation – the great secret, one so devastating that, if it were to get out, it would devastate the world—'

'—you said "devastate" already—' Robert put in.

'. . . would *destroy* the world's certainties,' Sophie said, 'upset Faith, erode social conventions.'

'All this from a *picture?*'

'Pictures can be very influential. They can have global reach. They can influence people in a hundred subtle ways. Think of the *Mona Lisa* . . . Leonardo's most famous image.'

'Ah yes. The original smiley,' said Robert, nodding. 'Only not so yellow. Or so circular.'

'What's interesting is that scholars are not certain who the image is supposed to represent. The name "Mona Lisa" is, for instance, a guess . . . Mona is short for "Madonna", and "Lisa" is supposed to refer to "Lisa Gioconda", the wife of a businessman. But there's no proof that explanation is correct. That information comes from Vasari, perhaps the least reliable historian in the history of history. Vasari was eight years old when Leonardo died, in 1519. He had no first-hand experience of the great painter. Most of what he wrote was hearsay – or, perhaps, deliberate misinformation. Do you know what the *Encyclopaedia Britannica* says about Vasari?'

Robert considered this. 'Is that a rhetorical question?' he replied, eventually. 'I mean, is it *likely* that I am going to know what the *Encyclopaedia Britannica* says about Vasari?'

'There's no need to be like that,' snapped Sophie. 'I was only going to cite your eminent national Encyclopaedia to support my assertion that Vasari is an untrustworthy source. They say "when facts were scarce, however, he did not hesitate to fill in the gaps with information of questionable veracity".'

'Right,' said Robert. 'Now I know what the *Encyclopaedia Britannica* says about Vasari. Which is, I'm sure, a good thing.'

'The point is that we cannot trust Vasari. We have no actual evidence that the so-called *Mona Lisa* represents a woman called Lisa.'

'Then why is it called the *Mona Lisa*?'

'My personal theory,' said Sophie, 'is that the title is a rude pun by Leonardo. We know he loved word games, puns, plays on words. We also know that he was a homosexual – he narrowly avoided prosecution for it on several occasions. I think the title "Mona Lisa" is a play on the Latin word *mōnaulēs*, which means "a player on the single flute".'

Robert thought about this. He pictured James

Galway. 'Well if that's a joke,' he said eventually, 'it's not a very funny one.'

'But don't you see? He was implying something quite suggestive. Most Roman pipes were cluster-pipes, like pan-pipes, lots of tubes together, called *aulus*. But the *mono*-aulus was an unusual pipe, just a single shaft. And by calling his painting a name that sounded like *mona-lees*, which is to say *mōnaulēs*, he was suggesting that the sitter . . . you know . . . "played" upon the single shaft of the "flute".'

'I don't get it,' said Robert. 'So she plays the flute. So what?'

'Not the flute,' said Sophie 'The "flute".' She made little quotation-marks gestures with her forefingers.

Robert thought about this until realisation dawned. 'Oh!' he said. 'Ah! I get it! That is quite rude. So is *that* why she's smiling in that mysterious way?'

'Well,' said Sophie. 'Possibly.'

'But,' said Robert, 'if the *Mona Lisa* is not a painting of some woman called Lisa, then who *is* it of?'

'It's not certain. But many scholars have noted a distinct resemblance between the so-called *Mona Lisa* and Leonardo's own self-portrait.'

'Not the beard, though.'

'No, not the beard,' Sophie conceded. 'But the strong, rather long nose; the knowing look in the eyes. The brow. Compare Leonardo's self-portrait and this painting, and you can't fail to be struck by how similar they are.'

'Are you saying that the *Mona Lisa* is actually a self-portrait of Leonardo?'

'Some people say so, a self-portrait in drag. But I don't think so. There are differences as well as similarities: the lower face and the mouth are quite different, for instance. But I'm saying that there is enough of a similarity to suggest a family resemblance . . .'

Realisation belatedly dawned for Robert. 'The *Mona Lisa* is a picture of Leonardo's *sister* . . . ?'

'Exactly. Once you look at it from that point of view, everything suddenly falls into place. Now, it was painted in 1500, when Leonardo was nearly fifty years of age; so clearly his sister was younger than he was.'

'Unless it was a deliberately idealised portrait . . . you know, flattering the sitter and so on.'

'Exactly! It was on this subject that I was corresponding with Professor Sauna-Lurker. To begin with he was a little standish-off . . .'

'Stand-offish?'

'Yes, that. Of course I understood why. There are many cranks and idiots in this line of enquiry, and man in his position cannot afford to waste time on . . . um, on timewasters . . . who would only, um, waste his . . . his time . . . but *recently* I felt he was beginning to trust me a little. He had got as far as suggesting that he and I should meet up. Indeed, he told me he had something very important to show me.'

'What? What did he want to show you?'

'I don't know. That meeting never happened. And now it never will. But if I had to guess, I'd say it was something relating to the so-called *Mona Lisa*, perhaps an alternate version of the image.'

'Alternate?'

'Yes. There are several copies and versions of the painting in existence today; that's well known. Some of those are later copies by students of Leonardo's. But there may be earlier versions of the image in Leonardo's own hand, or even – perhaps – a prior version of the image pained by Eda herself.'

'This is most exciting,' said Robert, jiggling up and down on his seat. 'I really feel like we're getting closer and closer to solving a really very exciting and mysterious mystery.'

'Here we are,' announced Sir Teabag. 'The National Gallery.' He pulled the car to a halt in front of the austere building.

15

There was still a police presence outside the gallery; a police cruiser parked across the pavement, yellow tape and two uniformed 'Bobbies'. As it happens, neither of them was called Bobby, but that's by-the-bye.

'We've got to find a way into that building,' urged Sophie. 'To get past those policemen and back to Jacques office. We need at least the *chance* of discovering whether the *Mona Eda* is still inside the Gallery.'

'Don't worry about the police,' said Teabag, with alarming panache. He pronounced the word "police" as if he wished to distinguish the 'Po' lease from some other variety of lease. 'I'll distract them. When they're distracted, run up the steps and break into the building.'

'Break in – how?'

'Just break a window why don't you?' said Teabag, 'warble wibble wobble. I assume, what with all the police wandering to and fro after hours, that they turned off the burglar alarm. Why should they need a burglar alarm anyway, when they've got a personal police guard outside the main steps?'

'Good point,' said Robert.

'Did you,' said Sophie, in a slightly troubled voice, 'say "warble wibble wobble" in the middle of that sentence?'

'Just getting into character.' said the Baronet. 'Distracting character. Police-distracting character.' He unzipped his tweed trousers and extracted his spaghetti-thin and spaghetti-coloured legs like a man defusing a nuclear warhead by removing the uranium core and ensuring it did not at any point touch the outer casing. Finally he stood there in the streetlight, unclothed from his boxers to his socks 'I'll dance past those policemen,' he said. 'When they give chase, it'll give you a chance to dash to that window there. Break the glass with a brick. Or anything. Get inside – that's the important thing. I'll try to give them the slip and join you later.'

Without further prevarication Teabag was off, frolicking and cavorting along the northside of Trafalgar Square, singing a song to the tune of *Una Paloma Blanca*, although with words of his own invention, the precise meaning of which Robert found quite hard to parse.

Sophie and Robert crouched at the foot of the Gallery's broad entrance staircase, peering round the stone balustrade at proceedings.

'That Sir Teabag,' observed Robert. 'He's quite eccentric.'

'He's more than eccentric,' said Sophie. 'He's XXX-entric. He's an adult-only oddball.'

Robert looked at her. 'That was another of your jokes.'

'It was,' agreed Sophie.

'It is rare for a non-native speaker to have sufficient fluency in English to be able, successfully, to make amusing jokes.'

Sophie looked pleased. 'You're flattering me!'

'Well, no,' said Robert. 'I'm not.'

'Oh,' said Sophie. 'I see.'

There was a difficult pause.

'But well done for trying,' said Robert, trying to be encouraging.

'Shush,' said Sophie. Sir Teabag had reached the police.

He did a little pirouette in front of the two impassive officers of the law. He continued singing. He pranced and danced away. The two policemen watched him, their expressions unchanging, as he frolicked away into the distance. But they did not move from their appointed posts.

'*Tiens*!' hissed Sophie. 'They are not going for it!'

'I guess,' said Robert, 'that drunkards or otherwise

brain-disordered pedestrians are not all that unusual in this neck of the woods in the small hours of the morning. Teabag'd need to do something more shocking to get them to actually leave their posts.'

Teabag was coming back down the pavement, past the policemen. This time the song he was singing put new and frankly upsetting words to Robbie Williams' popular hit *Let Me Entertain You*. Once again the police were unmoved.

Rather breathless, and with his legs a colder colour than they had been when he started, Teabag joined them behind the balustrade. 'Nothing doin',' he announced. 'They wouldn't take the bait. I baited them, but it was bateless.'

'What shall we do now?' hissed Sophie.

'It's your turn to run up and down without any pants,' said Teabag, in a petulant tone. Slowly, and with excessive care, he re-inserted his legs into his tweed britches. 'At any rate. It's set a chill in my lower limbs and no mistake.'

'I wouldn't run up and down there without my trousers,' said Sophie, demonstrating her impressive command of English-language popular idiom, 'on the end of a barge pole.'

'Wait!' said Robert. 'Listen!'

The police car radio was fizzing and crackling. One

of the two coppers hopped over, opened the driver's door, and leant in. In a moment he pulled his head out. 'They've gorrim,' he called to his partner.

'What does the word mean, the *gorrim*?' queried a whispering Sophie.

'The "t" mutates to an "r",' explained Teabag, 'under certain circumstances and in certain idio-lects . . .'

'Sh,' said Robert. 'I'm trying to eavesdrop.'

'They sure?' said Policeman Number 2, still stand-ing on the bottom step.

'Yep. Some guy called the Exterminator.'

'Exterminator!' said the second Policeman, im-pressed.

'That's right. With a moniker like that, he's bound to be in the frame for a job like this. They apprehended him in the Church of Our Lady of the Silver Scales in Blackfriars. They've video evidence that he was in the Gallery earlier, around the time of the murder.'

'Really?'

'Yep.'

'So what about that other feller, the professor chap? Him with the fingerprints all over the fish?'

'Sarge says there's still an All Cars out on him. He may be an accomplice. But he doesn't have the *form* for a murder like this. He's a penpusher. This other geezer, this "The Exterminator", Sarge says killing is his profession. He's the much more likely candidate.'

'Right,' said PC 2 'So do they need us here any more?'

'Nah,' said PC 1 with loud satisfaction. 'Why don't we pop down to that all night caff on the Chelsea Bridge Road and grab a cuppa?'

'Good idea!' replied his companion, equally loudly. They both clambered into their squad car and drove away.

Robert, Sophie and Teabag looked after them, hardly able to believe their luck.

'Did you hear that?' said Robert. 'They've arrested some chap called the Exterminator! I *told* you I hadn't handled that fish!'

'More important than that,' said Sophie. 'They have left the Gallery unguarded. Quick! Up the steps before they return! We must break in and search Jacques' office for clues!'

16

The Exterminator had indeed been apprehended. As he stepped from the Church, a bank of headlights dazzled him, and three uniformed policemen tackled him to the ground. 'Game's up, Exterminator!' called Inspector Charles 'Curvy' Tash of the C.I.D., striding over to where he lay, struggling, on the path.

'What are you bleeding playing at?' the Exterminator returned. 'Get your hands off me, Gladys!' he barked at the particular police constable who was trying to cuff him. The PC in question was not, of course, actually called Gladys. Rather "The Exterminator", by referring to him by this patently female appellation, hoped to call into question his masculinity, and thereby insult him.

'Ouch!' he cried. 'Watch it!' He was hauled to his feet.

'Bring him to the station,' ordered Tash.

17

Meanwhile, back at the National Gallery, the three intrepid investigators effected an entrance by breaking a side window with a discarded shopping trolley. It took all three of them to lift the trolley, and several goes before they co-ordinated their actions well enough to break the glass, but they managed it in the end.

No alarm sounded. 'Told you,' said Teabag.

They made their way through darkened exhibition spaces, and down the spiral staircase to the little hallway with the *Last Supper* mural. The door to Jacques Sauna-Lurker's office was open.

Sophie turned on the light, and the office was revealed to them in all its disarray. 'Come along,' Teabag urged, with a manic and rather alarming energy. 'There's got to be a clue here somewhere! Think cod. Think Jacques. Find something that the killer missed.' He strode into the snowdrift of paper.

'Do not worry, Sir Teabag,' said Sophie, confidently. 'We have with us Dr Robert Donglan, the premier anagrammatologist and clue-decipherer in the whole of London town. He can decipher any clue – can't you, Robert?' She looked intently at him.

'Well,' said Robert, nervously. He thought he detected a note of suspicion in Sophie's seemingly laudatory words, as if she were probing him, trying to determine just how good he was at solving clues. 'I mean, one doesn't like to boast . . .'

'Nonsense!' boomed Teabag, with exhausting jollity. 'Tell us the truth, man! Is Ms Nudivue's characterisation of you accurate?'

'Well I'm not sure about being able to decipher *any* clue,' Robert demurred. 'But, you know. One, *ahem*, does one's best.'

'He is professor of anagrammatology at the University of London,' Sophie informed Teabag. 'His modesty, though very English, is misleading.'

Robert looked at her, and his heart contracted with sheer love. She looked so beautiful, standing amongst the mess of paperwork, books knocked off shelves and upturned chairs; as if only mess could truly frame the neat pertness of her allure. When this crazy night was over, and the mystery cleared up, Robert thought to himself – then surely she would be prepared to go out with him? She was so committed to uncovering the great secret of this mysterious conspiracy; and if Robert could help her to that end, then surely she would be grateful to him . . . perhaps more than grateful . . .

But—

That terrible word! Small but obstructive, meaning as it does 'except' or 'except for the fact', or 'on the contrary', 'on the other hand', or even 'with the exception of', although that usage is less relevant here.

But, Robert thought, he had a secret of his own. A secret rooted in his past. And if Sophie were to stumble upon that secret, then could she do anything other than despise him? She thought him the greatest code-analyser in London, *but* . . .

As he stood in that office, Robert felt memory swimming up from those portions of his brain given over to the storage of memory, thoroughly italicising his thought processes . . .

18

The young Robert Donglan had been a typical schoolboy. Which is to say, he was almost entirely uninterested in his schooling. English was his best subject. A more precise way of stating that would be to say that English was his least awful subject — which is to say, although he was pretty awful at English he was considerably more awful at all the other subjects. His attention was continually wandering, as if on an endless pilgrimage to some ever-retreating intellectual destination. He spent a lot of time honing his 'staring gormlessly out of windows' skills.

His teachers despaired of him. He found it hard to take the conventional syllabus in. For many years he had believed that the noted Jacobean tragedy was indeed called Tis Pity She's A Whore Stop Giggling At The Back Jenkins. *He couldn't remember the differences between the three Lawrences, the DH (Mr), the TE (Mr) and the Merry Xmas (Mr). It bothered him disproportionately that the name of the poet Keats did not rhyme with the name of the poet Yeats. He could not say for certain whether Joyce was a surname or a first name. Nevertheless, when the time came for him to go to university (and it is a matter of Government legislation in the UK that all schoolchildren must go to university whether they like it or not) English was his least worst option, and so off he went to study for an English degree.*

'Study for' perhaps gives the wrong impression. If, by saying 'study for' I have given you the impression that Robert did any studying, or that he was in any positive sense 'for' the BA (Hons) English under the rubric of which he was notionally registered, then I'm afraid I have mislead you.

No: at university, Robert was an all-round scholar. By which I mean he was all round. He looked like one of those vast pale balloons that used to terrorise Patrick McGoohan on the beach at Port Meirion — same shape, same colour and, pretty much, the same consistency, only with a broad flat-topped head at one end. He spent his entire university career lying on a couch watching television, engaged in a marathon assault on the unofficial world record for 'largest amount of pork scratchings consumed over a three year period.'

Eventually his university career came to an end, and he had to work out what to do next. He paid a visit to the university career's officer.

'Donglan, is it?' said this individual, peering at his computer screen. 'It says here that you got a 2:2.'

'Does it?' replied Robert, adopting an expression of puzzled concern.

'Yes, not a very good grade, I'm afraid. That will restrict your employment opportunities.'

'Well that's a mistake,' said Robert, with a reasonably

convincing appearance of self-confidence. 'It's a typo. I've already been through this with the Registry. They said they'd already changed it on my official file. I'm rather annoyed to see that they haven't yet.'

'Oh!' said the Careers Officer, pleasantly surprised. 'Clerical errors do sometimes occur, of course. So what did you actually get?'

'A first,' said Robert. 'A starred first, in fact.'

'Congratulations! But,' and the Careers Officer's beaming face fell momentarily. 'But then why does it say 2:2 on your computer record?'

'It's an interesting story actually,' said Robert, smoothly. 'According to the Chair of Examiners, with whom I've discussed the whole matter, it's all down to a simple mishearing. There was a certain amount of celebration going on in the background, you see, high spirits and everything after the end of exams. People were drinking, dancing, singing songs; and one person – now, this is the crucial detail – had got hold of a 'Mr Toad® Brand Comedy Horn', and was blasting off with this from time to time. By unfortunate coincidence, this horn was sounded just as the Head of Department's secretary was dictating the list of final grades to the Academic Administrator. She said "Robert Donglan, Starred First" and the toot-toot of the comedy horn drowned out the last two words, becoming thereby inadvertently transferred into my official record. It's like,' Robert continued, 'the *opening sequence of Terry Gilliam's film* Brazil. *Do you know it?'*

'No,' *said the Careers Officer.* 'Is it good?'

'Terribly good. But more importantly, it is relevant to the present circumstance. If you could just correct the computer record from your terminal . . .'

The Careers Officer shrugged, but made the correction. 'Well I must say,' *he said as he typed in the password and tapped at the cursor keys to overtype 'starred 1st' in the box which previously contained the legend '2:2', 'I must say this is* excellent *news. I was going to suggest a career in retail. But with a starred first, all sorts of other possibilities are available to you. Have you considered a PhD?'*

Robert gladly embraced the prospect of three further years lying on a couch watching television and consuming pork scratchings. Indeed, he toyed with the notion of shifting snack-allegiance to something more challenging: hand-cooked 'sea-salt and balsamic vinegar' deluxe crisps, for instance.

And that's what he did. He began studying for a PhD in Modern Critical Theory. His supervisor was too busy jetting around the world to conferences on various exciting developments in the de-ontological metaphysics of the text to pay much attention to him. He registered for a thesis in 'Zizekian libidinal economies in post-Althusserian textual aporia', and then did nothing further until a few months before submission was due. Then, acting on a tip from a fellow and equally indolent PhD student, he generated his thesis by adopting the following practice: he went online and downloaded eighty-thousand words of German Philosophy in the original German. Then he put this text through an English spell-checker, randomly adopting the programme's suggestions for English words and thereby producing a text full of words proximate to the German ones in spelling, although often radically different in meaning. Then he divided this block of challengingly-syntaxed text into twelve chapters, cut-and-pasted the titles of eleven Zizek and three Althusser monographs randomly through the whole. This took him one afternoon. Printing it out and getting it bound took another two days. Then he went back to his couch.

By the time of his PhD viva, Donglan himself had slimmed down considerably from his undergraduate days, the result of a fortuitous combination of (a) discovering that he didn't like hand-cooked 'sea-salt and balsamic vinegar' deluxe crisps as much as he liked pork scratchings, and (b) the fact that he was too idle to get off the couch and go buy any of the latter. He bought a suit from Oxfam and responded to questions by nodding slowly and forming his eyebrows into '~~' shapes, before repeating a portion of the question back at the questioner in a very slow voice, rounded off with a 'yes, but we must not forget what Spinoza says regarding this'. The external examiner praised the dense, penetrating nature of Donglan's engagement with poststructuralist thought.

It was also relatively easy for him to get a job. He applied for a post teaching the thought of Jacques Derrida and modern critical theory. His suggestion, at interview, that he base his teaching on 'anagrammatology' was the result of his feeble memory struggling to recall the title of the one Derrida book he had heard of. But the interview panel were very excited by this new development in Derridean thought, and gave him the job. Since then it had been a simple matter of the teacher's Golden Strategy for masking ignorance: make the students do all the work.

But now! Now, for the first time in his life, Donglan was falling in love. Here was a beautiful woman, a no-nonsense, high-flying, power-dressing woman redolent of Frenchiness in all the best sense of that word . . . and she was interested in him! There was a chance! But—

But—

But — she believed him to be something he was not. She thought he actually possessed the finest critical brain in London. But he was a fraud! He had arrived at that position through no personal merit whatsoever. Could he keep up the pretence? Or would it be better to tell her the truth . . . to reveal all. But if he did so, would the love in her heart enable her to forgive him? Or would she spurn him as a spurnworthy thing? What should he do? Oh the dilemma! The terrible *dilemma! It was more than a dilemma — a trilemma. Or a dilem-Pa. No, that's a bit sexist, isn't it. I'm going to stick with trilemma.*

19

'Here's something!' cried Teabag. Robert was yanked abruptly back from his reverie, and his italicised memories of the past. 'I say, you two, I've found something!'

'What?' cried Sophie. 'What do you have?'

'Here . . . it's a piece of paper with your name on it, Ms Nudivue.'

'Let me see!'

But it was Robert, who happened to be closer to Teabag, who got first glimpse. 'This is odd,' he said, as Sophie waded through snowdriftlike paper to get to him. 'It's a print-out of a computer record. That's your name, Sophie, and that's your picture. But this describes you as a Computer Technician First Class in the Swiss-based multinational *Geneticon*. That can't be right, can it?'

'Another one of my undercover identities,' Sophie explained. 'I am convinced that *Geneticon* is deeply involved in the great mystery, one more high-tech front for the *Conspiratus Opi Dei*.'

'And are they?'

'My suspicions remain, although my actual investigations were inconclusive.'

'Do you mean unconclusive?' Robert asked.

'Isn't that the same thing?'

'Non-conclusive?' suggested Teabag, a sheaf of papers in his hands.

'Or is it disconclusive?' Robert suggested.

'I worked there for six months before my cover was blown,' said Sophie. 'In that time I became more and more convinced that not only *Geneticon*, but *all* the world's major computing industries are front organisations for the *Conspiratus*.'

'By golly!' exclaimed Teabag. 'I knew it! Computers are the devil's microwaves . . . but if the *Conspiratus* is truly the secret power behind all computing on this planet then the implications are terrifying . . .'

'I agree,' said Sophie. 'Pretty much every home has a computer now; the majority of the globe is connected to the world wide web. Any organisation at the centre of that web would be in a position of almost unimaginable power . . .'

'Deconclusive,' Robert tried. 'Anticonclusive. None of these sound right. I tell you what, perhaps we're coming at this from the wrong angle. Perhaps the opposite of *con*clusive is something like "clusive". What do you reckon? It might be one of those English words that exists but isn't used too often, like delible or domitable. Or sipid. I mean, shouldn't the opposite of *insipid* be *sipid*? Don't you think?'

Sophie and Teabag were looking at him in a strange way.

'Why are you looking at me like that?' he asked.

'What,' asked Sophie, 'are you *on* about? We can't hang about. We've got to find the clue that will lead us to the *Mona Eda* – and perhaps to the Holy Grail itself.'

'Right,' said Robert, stuffing the printout into his jacket pocket. 'Clue, yes.'

'It seems to me,' said Teabag, dropping the papers in his hand to join the pile on the floor, 'that the assassin has been through this office pretty thoroughly. I don't think we'll find anything in here to help us.'

'If only,' Sophie fretted, 'if only we could decipher this strange rebus with the 9 and the seeing eye that Jacques wrote on the mural!'

She stepped out of the office and into the hallway to look again at the strange message scrawled on the hairdo of Christ. Teabag and Robert followed her out.

20

'It's handsome, ain't it?' observed Sir Herbert Teabag, taking in the whole of the reproduction of Leonardo's *Last Supper* with a sweep of his hand. 'I was admiring it last month, when I paid Jacques a visit. He said he'd had to stump up for it out of his own pocket, since the Gallery wouldn't cover the cost of something nobody but the officer workers down here would see. But he didn't mind. He said the *Last Supper* was his favourite Da Vinci picture, and that it gladdened his heart to see this perfect copy of it every day, coming into work.'

Sophie was examining the mural in detail by putting her face close to the wall. As she looked at the lower elements of the composition this necessitated her bending forward. Robert was prepared to admit that the image was very attractive; but refused to concede that it was in any way as attractive as the sight of Sophie bending forward.

'D'you know what?' said Teabag, scratching his head. 'I asked him who'd he got in to do the painting . . . it's such fine and detailed work, you see. Not your regular painter and decorator quality. But he wouldn't tell me! Said it was a secret.'

'Eh?' said Sophie, standing up, to Robert's chagrin. 'What did you say? Did you say secret?'

'Yes.'

'But that's fascinating . . . because there are a number of crucial differences between this reproduction and the original in Santa Maria della Grazie. Look at the table.'

They all looked at the table.

'Loaves and fishes,' said Robert. 'That looks about right, doesn't it?'

'Well, for one thing the loaves and the fishes come from a different part of the New Testament,' said Sophie. 'That's the feeding of the five thousand, in Mark, Chapter 8. Not the *Last Supper*. And for another thing, if my memory serves me, there's only one fish in the original fresco, in the plate before Christ. I count *nine* fish on this table . . . and they're all different sorts of fish. Herring, monkfish, carp, sardine, pirhana.'

She looked again at the symbols written in blood.

Robert put his face close to the wall to look at the fishes, but overbalanced and smacked the bridge of his nose against the plaster. It made a dull, squelchy but very audible thud. 'Ow!' he said, standing up. 'Ah! Ow!'

'I have it,' cried Sophie.

'You have?' calloo-callayed a delighted Teabag.

'It is so obvious! Not to an ordinary eye, of course; but to somebody trained in the ways of the oblique rebus.' She turned to Robert. 'Don't you see? It's the theta that gives it away:'

$$9 \; \Theta \; \textbf{?} \; \circledcirc$$

'Of course,' said Robert, uncertainly, rubbing his nose. 'Gives it away. Yes.'

'You see – don't you? Now that I've given you that hint?'

Robert decided at that very moment, as his nose tingled unpleasantly and the electric light shone off the mural, to level with Sophie: to tell her the truth. Perhaps she would respect his honesty. 'Look, I think there's been a general over-estimation of my abilities as a code-cracker,' he said, rubbing his throbbing nose. 'I wouldn't so much as know what a theta *was*, not if it came up and thwacked me on the thigh.'

'Are you joking?' Sophie said in a puzzled voice. She pointed to the theta with her elegant forefinger. '*That's* a theta,' she said.

'Is it? I thought that was a little "H" in a circle. Like the sign for hospital.'

'It's theta, the eighth letter of the Greek alphabet. It represents a "th" sound. You must have known that!'

'I see. Th. Yes.'

'Well once you've got that,' said Sophie impatiently, 'the rest of the code falls inevitably into place. "9" for instance, in the Roman numerical system, is . . . ?'

Donglan waited for Sophie to finish her sentence, but it became apparent that she did not intend to complete it herself.

'. . . i-i-is . . .' she repeated, nodding at him with an encouraging expression.

Donglan looked at the ceiling. 'Is it "no"?' he hazarded.

'Don't be ridiculous. "IX" is nine. The question mark is clearly a rebus for the question "why?" – which is to say, the letter "Y". And the seeing eye is obviously "see" – or "C".'

'Or it could be "I" Robert suggested.

'But then the code wouldn't make sense. It's only when written out properly that it becomes clear what Sauna-Lurker was trying to communicate.' She reached into Robert's jacket pocket, pulled out his notebook, unthreaded the felt-tip pen from the rings of its ring binding, opened a new page and wrote:

$$I X \Theta Y C$$

Robert looked at this with the widened eyes of be-
lated recognition. 'Ah!' he said. He added 'ahhh!
Aahh! Aaaah!' on a rising series of musical tones.
Then he sneezed abruptly. His eyes returned to their
usual noncomprehending squint. He stared at the
word. 'Well,' he said after two full minutes had
passed, 'It's all Greek to me.'

'So you *do* recognise it,' said Sophie, pleased. 'I
knew it. I knew your "I'm an idiotic idiot" act was
only that – *only an act*. I knew nobody could be as
idiotically stupid as you were pretending to be! Of
course, you know perfectly well that the Greek letters
transliterate to—' and she turned the page and wrote
rapidly with the pen.

ICHTHUS

'Yes,' said Donglan, shaking his head.

'Of course,' said Sophie, 'Sauna-Lurker couldn't
write *that* on the wall. That would have been too
obvious.'

'Obvious,' echoed Robert. 'Ah!' Another sneeze
was building. He widened his eyes, and opened his
mouth. Sophie took this as a sign that he indeed
understood the full implications of what she was
saying.

'So he encoded it. But this—' she pointed at the pad with the felten-end of the pencil '—is what . . .'

'—ahh!—'

'. . . what he was trying to say. *Ichthus*. The Greek word for—'

'*Fsssssh!*' sneezed Robert, trying to stifle the explosion by pressing his hand against his mouth. This, however, only resulted in his getting a lot of saliva on his palm.

'Fish, exactly!' said Sophie. 'This was the word the Early Christians took as a shorthand for their faith. This is why they inscribed fish-shapes on their catacombs, and why some modern Christians put a fish rebus in the windscreens of their cars. Because Christ took his first disciples from amongst fishermen. Because Christ told his followers that he would make them fishers of men. So this word . . .'

'Aaah . . . *chthssss!*' sneezed Robert once more.

'Indeed – *ichthus* – yes, was taken as an acrostic, in Greek, the language in which the New Testament was originally written. Each of the letters in ICHTHUS stood for a Greek word in a significant phrase: I for *Iesus*, or Jesus as you say in English; CH for *Christos*; Th and U for *Theou Uios*, "the Son of God"; S for *Sotor*, or Saviour. If you were a Greek-speaking Christian of the first century, you read that phrase as easily as breathing, and you knew that "fish" meant "Jesus Christ the Son of God and Saviour". So there has always been this close relation between—'

'*Fsssssh!*' sneezed Robert one last time, with his hand before his mouth.

'—exactly! A close relation between fish and Christianity. The miraculous draft of fishes in Luke, Chapter 5! Christ's disciples being fishermen, and being made fishers of men!'

'Brilliant!' exclaimed Sir Teabag 'Of course!'

'Close relationship between fish and Christianity,' said Robert, rubbing his nose. 'Close relationship between *God* and *Cod.*' He sniggered. 'You get it?'

But nobody else seemed to be laughing. Indeed Sophie, so far from laughing, was looking at him with a prudish expression of shock on her face. This annoyed Robert. He didn't seem to be getting through to her at all.

'We have uncovered,' Sophie was saying, 'a secret of a profound nature . . .'

'And this helps us how?' said Robert, disproportionately annoyed with Sophie and Teabag's self-satisfied delight. 'It just looks like a whole lot of fish to me. Sauna-Lurker says "cod" in coughing-code over the phone; he writes "fish" in Greek, or rather in code-Greek, on a mural of the *Last Supper*. He dies with a great big codfish stuffed in his gullet. So what? *Where's the stand-up-in-court proof of responsibility for his murder?* That's what we're trying to find out — unless you've forgotten. The police have arrested this Terminator chappie, but they still think I'm an accessory. And nobody knows who this assassin was working for! And,' he continued, his indignation rising as he realised that he was bleeding slightly out of his bashed nose. 'And you'll forgive me for thinking that they won't be particularly impressed if I go along to them and say "alright coppers, you don't need to arrest me, I've got a whole bunch of fish references that prove my innocence". I mean, what *exactly* is the implication here? That Icelandic Cod Fishermen are responsible for Sauna-Lurker's murder?'

'You're not paying attention,' said Sophie, crossly. 'The fish is more than a fish. The fish is *Iesus Christos Theou Uios Sotor*. Don't forget what Jacques wrote on the wall upstairs: that the *Catholic Church* had him murdered. Not Icelandic Cod-fishermen. Fishermen of a different sort. For did not Christ tell his disciples "I shall make ye fishers of men? Is not the throne of St Peter called the Fisherman's Chair." '

'*That's* what the hook means,' said Teabag, pointing at the red three-quarters-circle added to the upward

pointing finger of St Thomas. 'It's not a reference to
Father Hook at all. It's a fishing reference.'

'I still don't see . . .' objected Robert, wiping his
nose on his sleeve.

'Look,' said Sir Teabag. 'Do you notice the detail
on the central fish? The one on Christ's plate?'

They all bent over and peered.

'Look at the fish's eye,' said Teabag excitedly. 'It's
been painted as a circle of black with a tiny white serif-
bar as the light-reflection in the middle.'

'It looks like a photographic negative of the Θ!' said
Sophie, excitedly.

'And the pattern of stippling around it makes it
look as though it is caught in the hook of a question
mark . . .'

'You don't think . . .' said Sophie with wild surmise.

'Let me try,' said Teabag. He reached forward, and
firmly pressed the cod's eye nine times.

After the ninth push, the eye clicked and recessed into the wall, drawn in by some whirring mechanical device. Then the entire figure of Christ, a triangular wedge of the composition that extended down through the table to the floor, snapped free of the composition, sunk half an inch into the wall, and then swung on hidden hinges away. A triangular doorway had opened in the middle of the mural.

'It's so obvious!' Sophie squealed with delight. 'This reproduction runs from ceiling to floor. But in the Santa Maria della Grazie in Milan the original is high up, *over a doorway* through which the monks went to and from their refectory. The implication is obvious; Jacques had this mural placed here as a way of saying, to those with enough knowledge, "there is a doorway *underneath* this image . . . a secret doorway leading down to secret underground vaults".'

'It is,' said Robert, peering into the musty smelling darkness of the newly opened doorway, 'as you say, obvious.'

'Come on,' said Teabag. 'I'll bet you a pound to a penny that the *Mona Eda* is down here . . . if it's down anywhere.'

'And who knows?' said Sophie. 'Perhaps the Holy Grail itself?'

21

They stepped through the small doorway one after the other. Sophie, luckily, had a small penlight; and using the wobbly circle of light this projected they made their way down a tightly curling circular stairwell.

'You don't think the assassin made it down here, do you?' Robert asked, somewhat nervously.

'It's unlikely,' said Sophie. 'Unless he was able to crack Jacques' code.'

'And there wouldn't be any, you know, Indiana Jones defence systems down *here*, would there?' Robert asked. 'Poisoned darts that shoot out of holes in the wall? Giant stones that roll down and crush us?'

'Who knows?' said Sir Teabag, behind him. He didn't help matters by laughing maniacally. His hilarity echoed disturbingly in the darkness.

Eventually they came to the bottom of the stairs. The walls disappeared; they were in a large underground space, smelling slightly of must and old books, and shrouded in pitch darkness. Or, since I suppose it is unlikely that many of those reading this narrative have any first-hand experience of 'pitch' . . . let me say instead shrouded in a darkness the same colour as a PlayStation2 console.

'Hmm,' said Sophie. The sound echoed slightly. She waved the penlight around, but it made no impact on the gulping darkness.

Robert decided to test the extent of the space in which they were standing, which he did by the traditional and time-honoured scientific process of shouting the word 'echo' as two distinct syllables in a slightly higher-pitched and considerably louder variant of his ordinary speech.

'-cho' returned the room.

'Wait,' said Sophie. 'Here's a light switch.'

Illumination flooded the cavernous space. Straight away Robert thought of the words from the Bible . . . 'Let there be light!' A thousand gorgeous works of art, sculpture and painting, tapestries and elegantly tooled leather bindings, were suddenly visible.

'Good gosh!' cried Sir Herbert Teabag. 'I feel like Carter in Tutankhamen's tomb.'

'There were carters in there were there?' said Robert, distractedly. 'What, to help schlep all the goodies out on big carts, was it?'

'No,' said Teabag. '*Howard* Carter, the archaeologist. He was the first person to see inside Tutankhamen's tomb, and when they asked him whether he could see anything he said "yes, wonderful things".'

'Did he now,' said Robert, not really following what Teabag was saying and instead looking wistfully after Sophie as she wandered through the treasures of this space. 'Did he really. Big cartloads eh, how interesting.'

It was a vast underground storehouse; hundreds of metres wide and long, and filled with sculpture, painting, books and other curios. 'Is this one of the official storehouses of the Gallery?' Robert asked. 'Is this where they store the exhibits they do not have space for in the actual gallery?'

'No,' said Teabag. 'This room doesn't officially exist in accounts of the Gallery.'

'A secret gallery!' said Robert, picking a dusty codex from a shelf. The spine carried the rather hiccoughy inscription *Att. Dell. Pontif. Acad. Rom. Arch. Correc. Cod. 1A xii*. This meant nothing to Robert. 'It's amazing!' he said. 'Astonishing.'

'But it would take us days to search all this properly . . .' complained Teabag. 'The *Mona Eda* could be any of these . . .'

'Here,' called Sophie, from the far end of the hall. 'I have found it.'

The two men hurried excitedly over. Sophie was standing in front of a canvas. 'The original *Mona Eda*,' said Sophie, with awe in her voice. 'Here it is.'

On the bottom spar of the frame was written one word: 'F.R.A.M.'

'So this is it,' said Sophie, in an awed voice. 'The *Mona Eda*.'

'What's *fram*?' asked Teabag.

'She's holding a fish,' Robert observed.

'A cod,' said Sophie. 'It's so obvious when you think of it! Every art critic who has ever written of this picture has remarked that it is modelled upon the traditions of Madonna painting – yet the Madonna is always portrayed cradling the infant Jesus – the Madonna and Child! The *Mona Lisa* sits there, smiling enigmatically, with her arms in cradling position, and yet she is cradling . . . *nothing*? Of course not! Now we know the truth. Leonardo copied this image, this self-portrait painted by his sister. He could not copy the cod, because that would have given, as you English say, the game away. So he simply painted out the cod, leaving his "*Mona Lisa*" incongruously empty-armed, leaving an obvious gap in the composition.'

'But—' said Robert, struggling to understand. 'I don't understand. Why a cod? Is it a reference to the *Conspiratus Whatsit Whosit* you were talking about earlier?'

'Of course not,' said Teabag. 'That acronym is specifically English. The Italian for "cod" is "merluzzo", and "*Conspiratus Opi Dei*" doesn't spell merluzzo.'

'So why a cod?' said Robert, his frustration becoming apparent in repeated little flappy gestures with his hands.

'The Holy Grail,' whispered Sir Teabag. '*Il calice santo*! This is the ultimate clue . . . this will lead us to it . . .'

Sophie had fallen silent, seemingly rapt in the

picture; yet still listening to the words that Teabag was speaking.

Indeed the Baronet was becoming more and more excited . . . 'I've long suspected it. Now this is the final confirmation! Jacques must have known too – and that was why he was killed! This is what he was trying to communicate to us, without letting his assassin know. This is it!'

'What?' cried Robert. 'For crying out loud! Will you just *tell me what all this means*, instead of beating about the bush for hours on end? Why does nobody speak straightforwardly?'

'You want me to speak straightforwardly?' said Teabag. 'Very well; I will explain in simple terms.'

And so, with both Robert and Sophie listening, he did.

22

Meanwhile, in Interrogation Room No 1, Hammer-
smith Police Station, the questioning of "The Exterminator" had reached a point beyond which further
questioning seemed rather pointless really.

'So,' said Inspector Charles 'Curvy' Tash, wearily.
'You admit that you were in the National Gallery
earlier this evening.'

'Yes!'

'But you deny any part in the murder of Monsieur
Jacques Sauna-Lurker?'

'Murder? I never murdered no-one!'

'Can you explain once again what you were doing in
the Gallery?'

'A little extermination job . . .' said the Exterminator. 'In the staff canteen, at the back of the building.
They'd been having a bit of bother with cockroaches,
so they called me in. I'd had a busy day, and only got
to the gallery fairly late. But all I did was lay traps for
the cockroaches, and then leave. I didn't murder
nobody!'

'And yet,' put in the sergeant, as if this were a
telling point, 'you are called "The Exterminator".'

'That's the company name, innit,' said The Exterminator. 'Central Office reckons it boosts trade to adopt the Schwarzeneggerean manner a little. People like to think that pest controllers ain't soft, see? They want their pests exterminated, not mollycoddled. But my name is Edwin, see? Ed. R. Herring of South Croydon. I'm no murderer! It's all a terrible misunderstanding.'

A third policeman entered the room, whispered into Tash's ear, and departed. 'Right Mr Herring,' said the Inspector. 'I'd like to thank you for helping us with our enquiries. It seems that footage from the security camera in the staff canteen has been analysed, and confirms your story. You are free to go.'

'At last!' said the Exterminator. 'I'm close to tears, I don't mind telling you. Me! A grown man! It's all been most trying, it really has.'

'Well, as I said,' repeated the Inspector wearily. 'We do apologise for any inconvenience. But I'm sure you can forgive our zeal, given the seriousness of the crime we are investigating.'

After the pest control man had left, Tash slumped in his chair. 'Bleeding wild goose chase!' he complained. 'Well it seems Mr Herring is not guilty of the murder of Jacques Sauna-Lurker after all.'

'Which means,' added the Sergeant, 'that the murderer is still out there . . .'

'Send out the squad cars. Put more men on the Gallery. Bring in reinforcements. We need to keep our wits about us. He could strike again at any time!'

'It's almost,' said his sergeant, 'as if this exterminator feller is a great red herring . . .'

23

'What do you know about the Holy Grail?' Sir Herbert Teabag asked his audience of two.

Sophie said nothing. Robert said: 'I *have* seen *Monty Python and the Holy Grail*. Is that any use? Can't say I remember any actual grails in that film though. I do remember the rabbit, however. And the knight who gets his arms and legs chopped off.'

'The Grail,' said Teabag, a little more loudly than was perhaps strictly necessary, 'was the focus for the legendary quests undertaken by the knights of King Arthur's round table.' The echo of his voice boomed mournfully around the chamber. 'A "grail",' he continued, 'is a kind of chalice, a wide-mouthed or shallow vessel; a cup in other words – scholars stress how common magic cups, or magic cauldrons, or magic "horns of plenty" are in pagan mythology. It's certainly possible that Christian myth picked up on pagan models and embellished them. The "grail" is supposedly the chalice from which Christ drank at the Last Supper, which was afterwards used to catch His blood during the crucifixion by Joseph of Arimathea, who later brought it to Britain. But it is not mentioned in the New Testament: it's first described by the twelfth-century poet Chrétien de Troyes in his unfinished romance *Perceval, ou Le Conte du Graal*. A great many later poets and artists have elaborated the mythos, amongst them Sir Thomas Malory's 15th-century prose epic *Le Morte D'Arthur*. In 1101 an Italian called Guglielmo Embriaco claimed actually to have recovered the Holy Grail itself during a Crusade to the Holy Land. It was supposedly a wide-brimmed chalice carved from a single gigantic emerald, and was displayed in the cathedral of San Lorenzo in Genoa; but later investigation discovered that the so-called Grail was actually a forgery, made from green glass. It has since been lost.'

'This is most edifying,' said Robert, politely.

'Most contemporary scholars,' said Teabag, examining the *Mona Eda* painting again, 'don't believe that the grail was ever an actual cup. They see it as, rather, a *symbol* of the truth and understanding needed to achieve the experience of salvation. More particularly, it is the vessel of Grace, the divine Grace of which Christ was the incarnation. In other words, it is *Mary herself* . . . for she was the vessel that carried Christ. The "chalice" becomes, then, a symbol of the Eternal Sacred Female Principle, the vessel that carries life and redemption within it. Do you see?'

'More or less,' said Robert. 'Um, what was the middle bit again?'

'Mary was the grail, and Christ himself the wine within it. Most Madonna-and-Child portraits are aware of this symbolism, and show Mary fully enclosing her child in her arms. Look at the Louvre *Mona Lisa*, and you can see that she has folded her arms around her lap in such a way as to almost make a seal: you can imagine pouring in fluid.'

Robert tried to imagine this. He looked at Sophie, but she seemed absorbed in Teabag's words.

'That is the problem with the "*Mona Lisa*", the Baronet continued, almost to himself. 'In her famous version, she is an empty chalice. It makes no sense. Madonnas are always painted with Child; the one *always* complements the other. The only exception to the rule is paintings of the Annunciation, when Mary is impregnated by the Holy Spirit, and even that subject is in a manner of speaking Mary and Child. But Leonardo's Madonna, his so-called "Mona" is clutching her arms around empty space . . .'

'Except . . .' said Robert, understanding Teabag's point, '. . . in *this* picture . . .'

'Exactly! This makes sense of everything! In this picture the Madonna is cradling her child . . . this

is the original that Leonardo copied, and bowdler-
ised . . .'

'Her child?' said Robert. 'But it's a fish. Shouldn't it
be a Christ?'

'In a sense it is a Christ,' said Teabag. 'Ichthus. I
suppose it's a sort of visual pun . . . or else—'

'Or else what?'

'Well . . . I suppose . . .'

'What?' urged Robert. '*What?*'

'No, the alternative is too extreme to contemplate.'

After a long silence Sophie spoke up. 'Is it?' she
said. 'Is it really?'

She turned to face them both.

In her right hand was a small pistol.

24

'Sophie!' exclaimed Robert.

'Mademoiselle Nudivue!' ejaculated Teabag.[1]

'What are you doing?' demanded Robert. 'You're pointing a gun at us!' He stopped for a moment, and then added: 'I appreciate that that sounds as if I have asked a question and then answered it, but my stating the obvious fact that you are pointing a gun at us does not actually provide an answer to the original question, which I therefore repeat: *what are you doing?*'

'Ha!' announced Sophie.

'Wait——' said Robert, with sudden relief. 'I know what's happening . . . this is a classic misunderstanding . . . we've both jumped to the conclusion that you're pointing that gun at *us* . . . when in fact you're aiming it at some enemy or adversary who is approaching stealthily behind us.' He looked behind

---

[1] [Publishers note: we wish to inform the public that we urged the author, Don Brine, to remove the phrase 'ejaculated Teabag' from his manuscript and replace it with 'said the Baronet in a wholesome manner entirely free from surreally obscene overtones'. Mr Brine declined to follow our advice, and in the subsequent long-drawn out lawsuit the Judge found in his favour. The text of the famous 'ejaculated Teabag judgment' is available at www.ejaculatedteabag.com]

him, but there was nobody there: only the precariously stacked items of art, the books and the curiosities. He turned back to Sophie.

'No,' she clarified. 'I am indeed pointing the gun specifically at you two. Hands up!'

Teabag and Robert put their hands up.

'But – but – but –', sputtered Robert, sounding briefly like a motorboat. 'But in heaven's name Sophie – why?'

'Why? Why am I pointing the gun at you? Because I intend to *shoot you both*!'

'Shoot us? What – to injure us?'

'Shoot you to kill you!'

Robert digested this. 'Again,' he said, '*why* seems to be the question that comes first to mind.'

'Do you mean "why shoot you as opposed to kill you in some other way?" Or "why shoot you rather than let you live?" '

'The second one,' said Robert.

'I'd be quite interested to know the answer to the first one too,' put in Teabag.

'Well,' said Sophie, stepping forward and moving the pistol between her two targets. 'The answer to the first one is that I don't have any more of those special genetically-modified fish to stuff down your throats; and that therefore a gun will have to do.'

'<gasp> *You killed Jacques Sauna-Lurker!* <gasp>' gasped Robert.

'Well I think that's pretty obvious now, isn't it? My work at *Geneticon* in Switzerland . . . which Jacques had only recently uncovered, incidentally . . . enabled me to breed a strain of fish in which your fingerprint was inscribed upon every scale. I smuggled eggs of this new breed out of the lab personally; I personally hatched and raised them in a pond not far from here. A pond in a London city garden; a house that belongs to *Conspiratus Opi Dei.*'

'*You are a member of the secret Consp . . .*' Robert began, with an even breathier gaspiness, but Sophie cut him short.

'Yes, yes,' she snapped. 'I think everybody has already worked *that* out. It should also be obvious that I carried one of those same fish in my shoulder bag when I came along to my appointment with Jacques Sauna-Lurker. *You* of all people should know, Sir Herbert, that I possess an almost freakish strength in my upper body. I wrestled you to the ground easily enough back at your house.'

'You did indeed,' recalled Teabag, almost wistfully. 'Before you slapped those chokers on my wrist. By "chokers",' he added, by way of clarification, 'I refer, of course, to the handcuffs.'

'Of course,' said Robert.

'My martial arts skills,' said Sophie, with a hint of pride, 'have been honed by the finest *Conspiratus* martial art tutors. I had no difficulty in overpowering poor Jacques . . . but he proved stubborn. He refused to tell me the location of the *Mona Eda*, even when I tortured him, marking his head with the Sacred Marks of the Gills . . .'

'Those cuts!' expostulated Robert. 'The cuts that were found on his body!'

'They have a profound and mystical significance in the secret teachings of the *Conspiratus*,' said Sophie. 'But Sauna-Lurker refused to tell me what I needed to know. I shoved him into his chair, behind his desk and started ransacking his office. But when I turned he had autodialed a number . . . in a flash I had leapt to him and punched him smartly in the chest. He coughed in pain, coughing into the telephone receiver. At the time I did not know the significance of those coughs, although now . . .' She smiled, self-satisfiedly. 'Then I dragged him to the centre of the room and thrust the cod down his throat. He knew he was finished. So I turned my attention to searching the room, leaving him choking on the floor. My back was turned for moments only, but I had underestimated his stubbornness. He crawled away, even though he knew he could not remove the cod . . . so he wrote the strange message on the *Last Supper* in the hall in his own blood; and then struggled up the stairs. I followed him, but by the time I got to him he was already dead. So I returned to the mural, and puzzled over the strange message.'

'That would explain,' said Robert, 'how you suddenly appeared as if from nowhere, in the middle of a Gallery surrounded by police in the middle of the night.'

'Of course. I heard the police arrive; and then I heard your voice. Imagine my surprise! After all the trouble I had gone to to frame London's most famous expert in codes and secret communication, here he was in person – brought in by the police. Thinking on my feet, I presented myself as a member of the Sûrité.'

'Did we ever get the answer to two?' Teabag put in.

'Sorry?'

'You remember . . . there were two things. One was "why shoot us as opposed to killing us in some other way?", which Mademoiselle Nudivue has answered with her account of breeding the specialist cod. But the other was "why shoot us rather than letting us live?" and I am interested in the answer to that question. I mean, I'd rather continue living, if it's all the same to you.'

'I'm afraid not,' said Sophie.

'But why?' pleaded Robert. Or pled Robert. Actually, looking at that written down I think I'll stick with 'pleaded'. '*Why* do you have to kill us? Come to think of it, why did you have to kill *Jacques*?'

'I'm afraid,' said Sophie, glancing at the painting behind her briefly, 'that you have both learnt too much. Monsieur Sauna-Lurker was on the verge of revealing the secret at the heart of the *Conspiratus* – the secret to which this painting oh-too-eloquently alludes. But it is a secret that my organisation has spent two thousand years keeping hidden. A secret too devastating for the world to hear. A secret,' she said, finally, 'the protection of which occasionally requires murder.'

'But you don't have to murder *me*,' said Robert, eagerly. 'I've absolutely no idea what the secret is.'

'I'm afraid I cannot take your word for that, my dear Robert; not when we consider that you are the world's leading expert in deciphering codes and uncovering secrets.'

'But that's the whole point!' said Robert, delightedly. 'I'm a complete fraud! I've absolutely no idea how to decipher anything at all! I tell you – those TV quizzes where you phone in an answer, and the TV company makes a fortune from premium rate phone lines by asking things like "who wrote *Romeo and Juliet*? Was it (a) William Shakespeare, (b) George Rattlearrow or (c) Brian Jiggleshaft" . . . those kind of quizzes, you know? Well I can't even work out the answer to *that* level of questioning half the time!'

'You'll forgive me,' said Sophie, in a chilly voice, 'if I don't entirely believe you. You knew that Ichthus was Greek, and that it meant "fish".'

'That was just sneezing!'

'You even knew the most secret formulation, the holy mantra at the very heart of the Secret Conspiratus . . .'

'No I didn't! No I don't!'

'You said it to me not five minutes ago! Pendant to the observation concerning the close relationship between fish and Christianity.'

'What,' said Robert flippantly, 'The Cod and God gag?' He tried a smile, but it faded from his face. Sophie was not taking his words as a joke. She was looking very sternly at him indeed.

'This is why I must shoot you! Both of you! You know too much. You know the Sacred Equivalence. There are people in our organisation, the Masonic Illuminated Mafia of Opus Dei Piscinum, who have worked loyally for decades and never reached a level high enough to be told the Sacred Equivalence!'

'What?' jabbered Robert. 'What? The Cod and God? You cannot be serious.'

'You said it again! You have spoken the Sacred Equivalence twice! If you were to speak it three times within the space of three minutes then . . . disaster will come down upon us. I don't know how you have come by this secret – you must be far cleverer and far more ruthless than I realised. I am tempted to shoot you right now, to kill you before you utter the blasphemous trilogy of Sacred Equivalences and bring disaster down upon us all . . .'

'I won't!' squealed Robert. 'I won't! Don't shoot!'

'But Jesus is only a fish in *symbolic* terms,' said Teabag. 'It's a metaphor. It's not *literal*.'

'Pah!' said Sophie. 'If you know the Sacred Equivalence, then you must know that it is far more than merely a metaphor. You must know it is *the literal truth* – the great secret apprehended only shadowly by human religions and philosophy.'

'Can I put my arms down now?' asked Robert. 'My hands are going a bit tingly.'

'No!' snapped Sophie.

'It's really quite tiring you know,' said Robert, tetchily.

'I don't care!'

'The muscles are aching.'

'You mean the Catholic Church is *actually* based on the worship of Cod?' said Teabag. 'Literally? The stuff that goes into fish fingers?'

'And now *you* are playing games,' said Sophie, dismissively. 'For you must already know the truth! You must know that only the *most senior* members of the Catholic Church are aware of the true basis of their faith. Once they are shown the Holy Grail they know the truth. But most ordinary Catholics are satisfied with the apparent meaning of the church. Most ordinary Catholics don't think twice about how completely their faith belongs to the Cod.'

'I really don't see . . .' said Teabag.

'How about if I put my hands behind my head?' suggested Robert. 'They'd still be up, you know, but I'd be able to rest my wrists on my shoulders . . .'

'Silence!' said Sophie. 'Keep your hands where they are!'

They twitched to attention, whilst Sophie paced all the way around them. She returned to the painting and looked at it again, tracing with the end of her pistol the sinuous path taken by the river on the left side of the image as it curls into the open bay.

'Water,' she said, almost to herself. 'Did you never wonder why the Christian faith is so involved with water? Water baptises a Christian into the faith. Why?

Jesus walked *upon* the water – water was his element; he mastered it completely. Water stands upon the left hand of Christ on the cross – the location of His kingdom. You are of course familiar with the identification of the four elements of the Aristotelian cosmos with the four arms of the Christian cross?' She sketched a cross in air with her gun, and then identified each of the elements by speaking them aloud and locating them with the pistol's end:

AIR

FIRE   ✠   WATER

EARTH

'Did you never wonder why Christ welcomed the especially blessed to his left hand? That is why. Christianity is the religion saturated in water. Or, to be more precise: human Christianity is obsessed with a harmony between the ocean and the land . . . between, as the Bible puts it, loaves and fishes.'

'None of this makes God a Codfish,' Teabag objected.

'How about if I moved over to the wall,' Robert tried, 'and sort of suspended my hands from something . . . take the weight off them? It really is quite uncomfortable holding them up like this all the time.'

'Look – do you want to hear my explanation of the whole conspiracy thing before I shoot you?' Sophie demanded. 'Or do you want to go whining on about how tired your arms are, so that I shoot you and you never get the bottom of things?'

'Well,' said Robert, stung, 'the former. I suppose.'

'Right. So stop whingeing and get with it. Now: Robert – specifically Robert. Not you Sir Teabag, you've answered enough questions already. I want Robert to try this one. What is the first thing that God does, according to your Christian Bible?'

Robert may have been a fraud as professor of annagrammotology, but even he knew the answer to that question. ' "Let there be light",' he said. 'Everybody knows that. First thing he says is "Let there be light". Then he divides the light from the darkness, calling the light Day and the darkness Night.'

'But *before* that,' pressed Sophie. 'You're right, Robert. Everybody knows that: "Let there be light". *Fiat lux*. But before he creates light, and day and night, and before he creates sun or moon or stars, or dry land, or animals, or man . . . *before any of that*, do you know what it says, in your Bible?'

'I have a feeling you're about to tell me.'

'I can recite it, word for word. Right at the beginning of *Genesis*. "Darkness was upon the face of the deep. And the Spirit of God moved upon the face of the waters. And God said, Let there be light: and there was light." ' She looked triumphantly at him. 'There it is – the clue of all clues! Hidden in plain sight at the very beginning of the single most read book on the planet!'

'The face of the waters . . .' murmured Robert.

'Exactly! The waters already existed, *before* God created anything else! It is even implied that the waters pre-exist God himself! Do you wonder that water is so important in Christianity? Water is the primal medium. Water is God . . . and the spirit of God moves *through* the waters before it moves *over* the waters.'

'You mean . . . ?'

'This powerful religious myth captures a crucial truth. Life began in the water. Your Bible tells of the creation of life *on the land* . . . but it records, right at the beginning, that the creation of the dry land is posterior to the existence of the Deep. Scientists have known this for centuries now: that life evolved first of all in the oceans.'

'Another thing,' said Robert. 'I mean, quite apart from the sore-arm thing, which is only getting worse, I might say – but I also need to go to the toilet.'

Sophie looked incredulously at him. 'The toilet?'

'Yes. To relieve,' he explained, with a slightly prim expression on his face, 'the pressure on my bladder. All this talk of water isn't helping.'

'Shut up. You'll be dead in a minute,' Sophie said, waving the gun at him.

'It's easy for you to say that,' said Robert. 'You're not the one about to wet his knickers.'

'What's the point in going to the toilet a moment before you die?

'Well, obviously, I'd rather not die on a full bladder.'

'Robert,' Teabag put in, 'could we go back to what we were talking about before please? It's really very interesting . . .'

'All I'm saying is that it's not a pleasant sensation, that sensation of a distended bladder.'

'If you can wait *just one minute*,' snapped Sophie, 'I'll shoot you dead and the unpleasant sensation will go away.'

'Ah but what if it doesn't?'

'What are you *talking* about?' cried Sophie, becoming more furious. 'You'll be dead!'

'But whilst I'm still alive . . .'

'Shut,' said Sophie, loudly, 'up!'

'Mademoiselle Nudivue,' said Teabag, 'if I may

just . . . you say that life evolved first of all in the oceans.'

'Yes,' said Sophie, turning back to Teabag.

'But not *intelligent* life!' Teabag objected. 'Unless you mean dolphins . . .'

'Dolphins!' sneered Sophie. 'Intelligent? Hardly. They are the dogs of the marine kingdom: eager, inquisitive, but no more intelligent than puppies.'

'Then . . .'

'Think!' said Sophie, almost savagely. 'Life has existed on the land for half a billion years. If you travelled back in time to the Triassic period, you would not expect to find intelligent life . . . dinosaurs, primitive mammals, rudimentary beasts, but no intelligence. Why? Because you know instinctively that intelligence takes many millions of years to evolve. This is why modern man is more intelligent than early hominids: because we have had more *time* to evolve. Time is the key! We don't know but that in another fifty million years maybe horses will become sapient.'

'Look . . .' Robert said. 'Can I hop on the spot for a bit? A little hopping from leg to leg might take my mind off the . . .'

Sophie ignored him. 'You *know* that intelligence is the result of evolution over long stretches of time! You *know* this! And where did life begin? In the oceans!

Which of life's kingdom's has had the longest period of uninterrupted evolutionary activity? The oceans! Life has existed there *twice* as long as it has on land! And if intelligent beings can evolve on land over half a billion years, then does it not follow logically that beings twice as intelligent would have evolved in the oceans in twice the time?'

'I think I see what you're saying,' said Teabag. 'But I think also I see the flaw in your reasoning.'

'There is no flaw! Or did you say floor? Because there *is* a floor to my reasoning – the very bedrock of truth itself. But no flaw, eff-ell-ay-double-you.'

'The eff-ell-ay-double-you in your logic,' said Teabag, 'is that intelligence in an animal must manifest itself – there must be evidence, you know. But where *are* the marine humanoids? How often do trawlermen dredge up talking creatures? Where are the undersea cities?'

'We are talking,' said Sophie, a little prissily, 'about an intelligence *far in advance* of humanity. Can you imagine how advanced human beings will be in a billion years? Were such a person to travel back through time he or she would seem to us nothing less than a god. You ask where are the cities: I say they are well hidden. You ask why does intelligent sea life not get snagged in fishermen's nets . . . I say to you, this life is intelligent enough to be able to avoid such a fate.'

'But . . .' said Teabag, 'but *thinking cod*? . . . it beggars belief.'

'More than thinking . . . much more . . . the creatures you call cod are actually beings of transcendental wisdom. They are the gods of this world. They invented computers millions of years ago – why else do you think computers operate in binary code? Has it never occurred to you that a computer invented by a ten-fingered human inventor would operate according to a ten-point code? Computers operate in binary because cod count in binary; not ten fingers but left fin, right fin.'

'Well that's just bizarre,' said Robert. 'And I might just point out, my hands are really tingling *really quite a lot* now, what with having been held up for so long.'

'They have a plan for us,' said Sophie. 'They are guiding us on an upward path. From time to time they release some new piece of technology into the human realm . . . computers are a good example. They are as far above us in intelligence as gods!'

'But human fishermen haul them out of the sea in their millions!' said Teabag. 'We eat cod! We turn them into fertilizer, for crying out loud! If cod really were so much more intelligent than us, wouldn't they stop us?'

'Indeed,' said Sophie. 'But the little fish men take from the oceans – those aren't fully developed cod. They are more like . . . let us say, like spermatozoa. They throng the oceans in their mindless way; but only one or two of each year's multitude goes on to develop into a fully adult, intelligent Cod: forty metres long, densely packed with muscle and brain, living in vast cities hidden on the oceanic floor, whose beauty and complexity you cannot even begin to fathom!'

'Sperm?' repeated Robert, with some distaste, thinking of all the fish fingers he had eaten in his life.

'Do the real Cod care about the loss of so many millions of the immature fish? Do you care if one or two, or even if millions of your spermatozoa are wasted? Of course you do not.'

'But where *are* these great cities of which you speak?' demanded Teabag.

'Hidden away from the prying eyes of humans,' said Sophie. 'Deep within oceanic trenches at the bottom of the sea.'

There was a pause.

'This picture,' said Sophie, turning to look at the painting, 'if it ever saw the light of day, would lead scholars along the same path that you have yourself trodden. They would uncover the truth about Eda Vinci herself; her membership of the *Conspiratus Opi Dei*. The secret at the heart of that organisation. The Sacred Equivalence itself. The location of the Holy Grail. That was why I was ordered to find this picture . . . to take it away with me back to Avignon, the European centre of the C.O.D. You can imagine my frustration when, even after torturing and killing Sauna-Lurker, I was still unable to uncover its hiding place! And so I must thank you both . . . without your help I would never have made my way into this secret underground storage space. I pretended to share both your interests and your ignorance; but now that the truth is revealed I must kill you.'

She pulled the *Mona Eda* from its place on the wall, and moved it over to the doorway. As her attention was momentarliy diverted Teabag leaned a little way towards Robert. 'She's made a fatal mistake! The common error of the criminal mastermind!' he hissed.

'I used to fancy her, you know,' Robert whispered back, mournfully. 'I was going to ask her on a date.'

'She couldn't resist telling us all about her evil plan! That means she's given us time to formulate a counter-attack! It's a schoolboy error!'

'A date! Really I was. Not any more though,'

Robert whispered. 'I'm prepared to put up with a lot in a woman: nagging; poor dental hygiene; uninterest in sports; cuddly toys on the bed. But the one thing I am really *not* prepared to put up with is trying to kill me. Call me fussy if you like.'

'Never mind that now,' hissed Teabag. 'We need to coordinate our counterattack! Before she kills us and gets away with the picture!'

'What counterattack?'

'The one we've been formulating whilst she's been telling us the terrible secret behind her crime!'

'But I haven't been formulating a plan of counter-attack,' said Robert. 'I was too busy listening to what she said, about the Cod being God and living in hidden cities under the ocean with computers and everything. Didn't *you* formulate the counterattack plan?'

'My dear fellow,' hissed Teabag, 'I really don't think it's fair to expect me to do all the work . . . we're in this pickle together . . .'

'Well what are we going to do?'

'Maybe her talking has occasioned just enough delay for a surprise rescue by a third party – oh no! Here she comes . . .'

'What,' said Sophie, the gun levelled at the bridge of Robert's nose, 'what are you two whispering about?'

'We were just,' said Teabag, 'discussing the fascinating details you were just regaling us with.'

'We were,' said Robert. 'Talking about fish. Not about planning our escape, or anything like that. Definitely about fish.'

'Escape! Hah!' said Sophie. 'Escape is impossible, I regret to say.' She raised her pistol, aimed at Robert, and began squeezing the trigger.

'Wait!' said Teabag. 'You can't shoot us yet! You've told us a great deal about the secret of the *Conspiratus* . . . but not everything. What about the location and indeed the true nature of the Holy Grail? You haven't told us about that, now, have you? It'd be an awful shame to kill us before telling us that . . .'

'He's right, you know,' said Robert. 'That's something of a loose end, wouldn't you say?'

'The location of the Holy Grail,' mused Sophie. She glanced behind her at the picture. 'Well, I'd love to fill you in. But, truth to tell, I'm a little tired of all this expostulating.'

She aimed the gun at Teabag and pulled the trigger. Robert dropped his arms and flinched two steps back. The noise in the confined space was so shocking, so ear-punching, like a thick sheet of metal being ripped rapidly into two pieces by gigantic hands, that it seemed to overwhelm him. He staggered on his feet as if he were the one who had been shot, and hid his face in his hands.

Teabag went down like a fairground target. He had been shot in the stomach.

Robert, uncoiling from his instinctive flinch, smelt the tang of cordite in the air, and looked to Sophie. Cordite is an explosive propellent made from two chief ingredients, nitrocellulose and nitroglycerin, to which has been added in most common contemporary cordites nitroguanidine. As well as being used in fire-arms, it has been used as a rocket propellent. The name comes from an early version of the explosive, created by British inventors Sir Frederick Abel and Sir James Dewar, who mixed 58% nitroglycerin, 37% gun-cotton and 5% vaseline in 1889. This material was extruded in spaghetti-like strands during manufacture, and therefore called 'cord powder', which was then abbreviated to 'cordite'. It's interesting, this, isn't it? Not that I want to destroy the narrative tension or anything.

So – Robert looked at Sophie. Her face was impassive. A shoestring of smoke curled upwards from the pistol, catching the electric light along its palely sinuous length. Then he looked down at Teabag. There didn't seem, at first, to be much blood, although there was a bit of a mess on his waistcoat, near the two bakelite buttons, it didn't look worse than a bit of dark gravy that might have been splashed onto his front by a careless waiter at his club.

'Teabag!' he cried, aware as he spoke of how stupid this would sound to somebody coming fresh upon the scene and unaware of the Baronet's name.

'Oh I've been shot,' groaned Teabag, looking up at the ceiling. This statement seemed to agitate him, for he twitched, grimaced and began to struggle on the floor. 'Stupid!' he said. 'I'm *such an idiot*! I'm going to die, and is that – *really* – the best I can do for last words? Idiot!'

'Teabag, don't exert yourself . . . we'll get an ambulance,' said Robert. 'Lie still and try not to . . .'

'Nobody's going to put old Teabag into *The Oxford Book of Famous Last Words* on the basis of "oh I've been shot" are they?' fretted Teabag. Blood was coming out of his nose. He tried to turn on his side, but the pain made him gasp and cry, and he slumped back onto his spine. 'Oh this is *most provoking*,' he said. 'It really is.'

'Teabag, please be quiet,' urged Robert. He started towards the supine Baronet, but stopped at a single shake of Sophie's head, and the sight of the gun aimed squarely at his own midriff. 'Whatever you do, don't say anything else. Lie still!'

'I've had a whole lifetime to think up some really

interestin' famous last words, and all I can manage is *"oh I've been shot"*. It's pathetic!'

'Come now my dear friend,' said Robert. He surprised himself; for tears were itching in his own eyes. Blood was much more evident now; expanding blackly onto the floor like ink being fed by capillary into a stretch of blotting paper. The dust of the old storage space seemed to be sucking Teabag's blood up with unpleasant eagerness. 'Come now, "oh I've been shot" aren't your last words. You've said several things since you said "oh I've been shot". Your last words after all are the *last* things you say. That's true by definition.'

'I suppose that's right,' said Teabag, in a milder voice, a little mollified. A painterly line of red came out of each nostril, and veered away from the mouth to mark a passage down the side of the Baronet's head. Then he convulsed again, his face rictusing in disgust. 'But, but that's *worse* – now my last words will be *I suppose that's right* – that's not any better than *oh I've been shot*. In fact it's much worse. That's so insipid! I mean how likely is it that in future centuries people will say to one another, "you know Herbert, twenty-seventh Baronet Teabag? His last words were *I suppose that's right*." It's not memorable is it – hurgh! Hurgh! Hurgh!' He did not, I should add for the sake of clarity, *say* those last three words. They are intended to represent his coughing, coughing which not only put his lungs into spasm, but produced spatters of be-spittled blood from his mouth. 'Oh why can't I think of famous last words worthy of me?' he gasped.

'That's it!' said Robert, eagerly. 'Those will do! They're perfect – clever and self-referential, simultaneously representative of the high standards of your inquiring mind, and also of the postmodern logic of contemporary existence in which it is not the profundity of a statement but its deconstructed irony that embodies the spirit of the age. "Oh why can't I think of famous last words worthy of me?" works brilliantly as an ironic commentary on the impossibility of profound statement in the postmodern world.' Teabag started to say something else, but Robert cut across him. 'No, don't say anything else, old boy. Don't spoil the moment . . . you've come up with the ideal last words.'

Teabag groaned.

'Not another *word*, my friend,' said Robert, forcefully. 'I insist.'

And so Teabag didn't say anything else. As it happens, ever again.

An unnatural silence settled into the little space.

Robert turned to Sophie. 'You monster!' he said, heatedly. 'You've killed a Baronet!' His outrage momentarily overcame his natural timidity. 'I won't let you get away with this,' he vowed. 'I'll make sure that—'

Sophie shot him.

Robert Donglan's first sensation was one of surprise and indignation rather than pain. It felt as if somebody had thwacked him very hard in the solar plexus with a baseball bat. Or a 'cricket racquet', the large wooden racquet not unlike a thickened baseball bat used in the game of cricket, a game with which, as an Englishman, Robert was obviously well acquainted.

He was sitting down on the hard floor. He couldn't remember sitting down, and yet down he was. The blow to his stomach had winded him, and the breath wasn't coming into his lungs very well. He was looking up at Sophie now as she stood over him. He was aware of the coldness of the stone floor beneath his thighs; he could feel it through the rather thin material of his trousers. There was a wetness soaking into that same fabric, touching his right leg with a sensation of rather clammy moisture. He still couldn't seem to draw a breath. He must have sat down into the pool of blood that had spilled from Teabag's wound. Except, putting his hand to his stomach he encountered a whole mess of wetness, throbbing out and pouring down into his lap and down each leg. So he had probably sat down in his own blood.

He wanted to say 'that's not good', but didn't have the breath for it. The blow to the back of his head puzzled him. But he realised, with a little thought, that he had slumped backwards from his sitting position, and was now lying on his back. And that was the last thing he remembered.

25

Robert drifted in and out of consciousness. A sensation of pain grew in his gut, magnifying from ache to intense discomfort. He tried to sit up, but the wrenching of torn muscle and shredded nerve-ending resounded agonisingly through his whole system. He gasped, and moaned. Everything was dark, woozily saturated with pain. He felt acutely thirsty. Everything blurred and went away, but even in a state that could by no means be described as conscious Robert was aware of the extraordinary pain in his gut. It howled through his body.

He regained consciousness again. There was a voice – somebody he recognised. In his shattered and agonised state it took him a moment to understand who was speaking. Father Hook! The priest had regained consciousness, and had followed the clues to the National Gallery. He had come to rescue them.

'Teabag!' Robert heard the priest exclaim 'And you – the other chap, whose name I'm afraid I've forgotten, although to be fair to me I only met you for the first time this evening! Both shot? Alas – I've arrived too late!'

Robert heard a second voice; the melodious, slightly lilting, barely francoaccented voice of Sophie. 'I'm afraid you have, Father Hook. Too late for them. Too late for you!'

Robert could see nothing. Everything was a dark blur. He felt so abominably *thirsty*. His head was faint, and chimed hideously with the pain in his gut.

'You!' he heard the priest exclaim, somewhere a few yards away that was also a million million miles distant. If you see what I mean.

'Yes,' came Sophie's voice. 'Me.'

'So it was you that murdered Jacques! And now you've finished off Teabag and the other one! You fiend!'

Sophie only laughed.

Robert could feel consciousness slipping away. He held on to his thoughts, fighting the slippage into the void. He had to help Hook in some way! Warn him . . .

'But *why* did you kill them all?' demanded Hook. 'Tell me why?'

'Well,' said Sophie. 'I could explain it all. Actually, I'd quite like to. Only I've already explained the whole shebang to those two . . . and now that they're dead I'm wondering to myself why I bothered. I mean, it takes quite a time to say it all, and now my mouth is all dry. So I'm afraid I won't be able to explain anything to you before I . . .'

The sound of the shot jarred Robert awake. It was immediately followed by the sound of a body slumping onto the floor.

His gut-pain was relentless. With enormous effort Robert lifted his left hand to his tummy; everything there was wet and warm. He rested his hand and his middle finger flopped into a cavity. It was the bullet hole. It didn't hurt Robert to put his finger into his own wound – at least, it didn't hurt him any more than he was hurting anyway; since he was hurting an immense amount. But it was weird to feel his finger waggling inside his stomach, to feel the thickly ragged rim around this unnatural addition to his body's holes. He could feel on his finger the pulsing wash of blood coming out of his body. He was crying. Real, hot baby tears were coming out his eyes. It was so unfair! The pain just kept on and on. He kept expecting it to diminish, for the edge to go off it, even if only a little bit. But it just ground away and ground away. There was no appeasing it. Please, he begged, although he was not sure whom he was begging. Please just let me pass out.

He passed out once again.

26

But it didn't do him much good though, because he came-to again. Although he had been unconscious for fifteen minutes, it felt to him as if there had been no passage of time.

The pain was still intense, agonising, and the thirst was worse. He felt dizzier, more distant. This was no good at all. This was not in the slightest bit good. He tried to contract his muscles, to drag himself across the floor – with no clear idea at all where he was going – but his muscles flat refused to obey him. The whole cosmos had shrunken to the radiating, pulsing agony of his gut.

More voices. It took him longer to work out who was speaking. The female voice was Sophie. He knew that. There was a male voice as well. It sounded familiar, but he could not place it at once. Then it clicked, in between throbs of agony. The policeman! What was he called? Tash – Tash – that was it. The police had come!

Robert felt a surge of hope in his shuddering heart. They police would arrest Sophie. They would get him medical attention – blood transfusion – morphine.

He tried to tune in to what was being said.

'. . . don't know where the priest came from,' Sophie was saying. 'The last thing I knew he was unconscious in Teabag's house.'

'He regained consciousness in the ambulance,' came Tash's voice. 'According to the report we heard. He insisted they stop, that he get out. Then he came straight here.'

'I had to shoot him, I'm afraid,' said Sophie.

'Of course.'

'I apologise.'

'Don't apologise,' said Tash. Both the voices were much closer to Robert's location now. 'This one here – he might just as well have shot two men as one.'

Somebody was taking Robert's hand, lifting it and curling the fingers around a cold, hard, angular object. A gun! Somebody was putting a gun in his hand!

He struggled to lift the gun and fire, but his muscles felt nerveless, dead. The hand was laid down on the floor.

'We've the fingerprint evidence, and the shooter,' Tash was saying. 'Our wild goose chase with the bug exterminator gave you enough time to extract the secret of the code from these three. So we located Sauna-Lurker's secret stash.'

'Am I to be included in the investigation?' Sophie's

voice asked. She sounded closer. As if she and Tash were now standing over Robert's body.

'No, I don't think there's any need for that. You'd better get this *Mona Eda* painting out of the country. Diplomatic bag. We'll pick up the loose ends, my dear, don't worry about that. I returned to Gallery – I heard shots downstairs – I came down to find that Donglan had killed Teabag and Hook, but that Teabag got him with one shot before dying.'

'And the ballistics . . . ?'

'The ballistics people are *Conspiratus* too. Most of the City of London Police are. It's like the Masons. This, after all, is the ancient City of the Fish. If people would only look at the map of the City they'd realise that!' He chuckled to himself. 'No, Mademoiselle Nudivue, I wouldn't worry about that. The report that comes out of ballistics will match any story we choose to make up.'

'Then we're done here,' said Sophie.

'I think we are.'

'Poor fellow,' said Sophie, after a slight pause. 'He really had no idea.'

'How close did he come to the secret?' Tash asked. 'Did he divine the location of the Holy Grail?'

'The Fram Trench? The deepest portion of the Arctic ocean, over seven thousand meters deep and almost wholly unexplored by man? No,' said Sophie. 'Teabag and he were still thinking only in metaphorical terms. "The Madonna is the grail", "the female principle is the grail", that sort of thing. It really didn't occur to them to think not only *literally* but on the *largest scale* . . . a container for fluid, yes – one that contains *a whole sea*! A container in which God lives . . . literally so, for the city of the Holy Cod is located there, thousands of square miles of underwater city, in which the greater pressures of the deepest ocean is moderated by advanced Cod technology to allow the civilisation of the Master Species to live their comfortable, transcendent lives. The *true* Holy City! The incomprehensible urbus! Humans will continue to look either for a cup, or something symbolic. The grail-shaped ocean depression in the Oceanus Hyperboreus is too obvious for them.' She sighed. 'I almost feel sorry for them.'

'No need to feel sorry for *them*,' said Tash. 'They're all dead.'

Sophie laughed at this, and Tash joined her. Most unpleasant, really. Uncalled for.

It was the laugher that did it. Waves of almost overwhelming exhaustion, pain and nausea coursed through Robert's agonised body; but he felt his willpower condense into a sparky point in his breast.

There was a tingling in the otherwise paralysed muscle of his arm. The two of them were still talking.

'Have you had a chance to explore this little cache of hidden items?' the man was asking.

'Yes. In the quarter of an hour that it took you to arrive I had a good look around.'

'Is there any other incriminating material? Anything else we ought to remove to the *Conspiratus* head-quarters in Avignon?'

'Not really. Apart from the *Mona Eda* itself. And a notebook in which Eda Vinci seems to have spelled out the true nature of the *Conspiratus* itself . . . very rash of her. But nothing else apart from those two things. And once we've removed those two items there will be no evidence here of the true nature of the C.O.D.'

Robert was exerting himself as he had never exerted himself before. Although almost no part of his body moved, it took every scrap of willpower he possessed. He strained. His right forearm contracted minutely. The pain in his gut continued to rage.

'And where are those two items?'

'I put them over by the door. I'll get them in a minute. Or do you want to get your Sergeant to trans-port them to a safe house for the rest of the night?'

'No, the Sergeant is a regular policeman. Not a part of the *Conspiratus*. I told him to wait in the car, to call for backup. We don't want him to see any of this material.'

Robert heaved again, and his forearm muscle contracted a little more. The weight of the gun increased in his hand as he lifted it millimetres off the floor.

'Then I shall take those two items myself,' said Sophie, her voice close by Robert's right. 'It would certainly not do for them to become generally known.'

'Yes, take them away,' said the policeman. 'We must at all costs ensure that non-*Conspiratus* people do not stumble upon them.'

There was the slightest scraping noise, as the stock of the pistol dragged gently against the floor. Robert had managed to swivel the gun in his hand through ninety-degrees, so that it was now pointing upwards.

'I say, Sophie,' said Tash, putting in his own personal entry for inconsequential last words. 'Are you sure he's actually d—?'

The pistol fired once, twice, three times. The recoil snapped painfully back against Robert's angled wrist, but he hardly felt it. His grip on the gun wobbled and he almost let it slip, but he was just able to recover it and fire again a fourth, a fifth, a sixth time. With each shot the gun jolted and repositioned itself, effectively spraying the space above him with six different trajectories.

There was a pause.

Then there were two thuds, one to Robert's left and one to his right, such as might be made by two bodies hitting a stone floor.

Robert let the gun go. The urge to fall asleep was impossible to resist. As he slipped into unconsciousness, uncertain whether the thudding he could hear was the sound of footsteps coming down the staircase or a migraine-like banging inside his own skull, he thought he could smell – impossibly – the smell of something . . . fishlike . . .

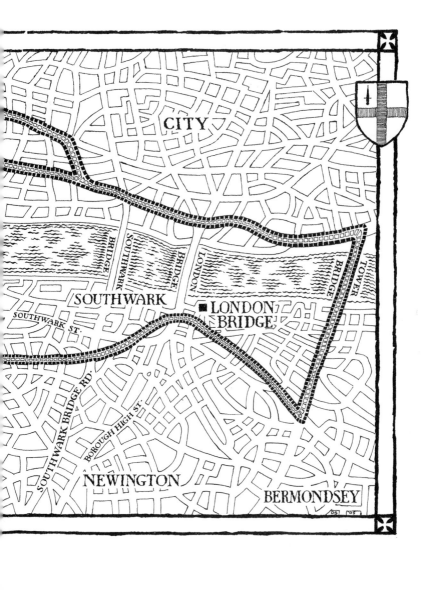

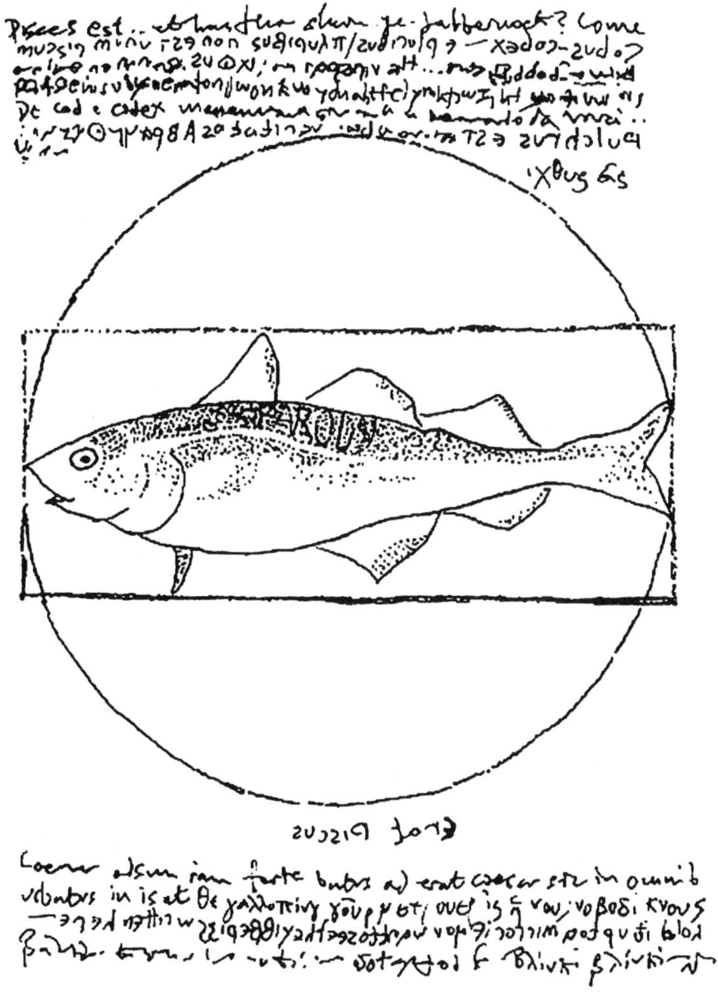

Pisces est ..
De cod e codex